Fundamentals of Criminal
Justice Research

Fundamentals of Criminal Justice Research

Robert S. Clark
Florida International University

Lexington Books
D.C. Heath and Company
Lexington, Massachusetts
Toronto

Library of Congress Cataloging in Publication Data

Clark, Robert S. 1916-
    Fundamentals of criminal justice research.

    Bibliography: p.
    1. Criminal justice, Administration of—Research. I. Title.
HV6024.5.C63   364'.07'2   76-28675
ISBN 0-669-01005-7

Published simultaneously in Canada.

Printed in the United States of America.

International Standard Book Number: 0-669-01005-7

Library of Congress Catalog Card Number: 76-28675

To Ciel

Contents

List of Figures

List of Tables

Foreword

Undoubtedly, the future will shock law enforcement with unimagined challenges. But in many respects the police world has already been invaded by currents and movements that have drastically upset its hallowed traditions. No wonder that police administrators grow desperate as they contemplate the enormous difficulty of fulfilling their responsibilities.

And paradoxically, a significant portion of that malaise in the ranks of the law enforcement institution emanated from a beneficient organization. Established in 1968 to prevent/reduce crime and to improve the criminal justice system. The Law Enforcement Assistance Administration (LEAA) proved to be a cornucopia that lavished two-thirds of its budget billions upon the police agencies of our country. LEAA accomplished a dramatic revolution by: stimulating managerial experiments and improvements; providing futuristic technology, especially computers; escalating educational programs for police personnel; infiltrating with a variety of research projects; and always insisting upon equal rights for women and minorities. All this within eight years in an occupation that had successfully and persistently resisted fundamental change.

During this period all the problems of urban police departments have become swollen. Great cities, facing bankruptcy, not only are thinking the unthinkable, but also are doing it by reducing the size of their police forces and decimating the police budgets. Finally, crime has continued to increase so inexorably that the very basic function of the police—crime prevention—is called into question.

Under these emergency conditions the venerable cloak of police secrecy has been ripped to shreds. And police officials can no longer hide behind platitudes or appeals that rely on the pervasive fear of crime to gain their ends. Police administrators are on the firing line: allegations of corruption must be investigated, budgets must be defended against city economists who want to amputate, patrol practices must be justified when attacked by researchers testing the null hypothesis that variation in type of patrol makes no significant difference in crime rates. Robert Clark's *Fundamentals of Criminal Justice Research* will stockpile an arsenal as a bulwark against these assaults. Steered skillfully by the author, the reader can avoid falling into "Type 1" or even "Type 2" error, the traps of fallacious argument.

The growth of police unions has added one more complication to police administration. No longer are the chief and the top echelons equivalent to Olympian gods with unchecked power over the members of the force. What subordinate dared question a decision or an order? Now before a superior orders men to emergency duty, he must first check the union contract provisions, compute the cost of overtime pay and obtain permission from the union representative to alter assignments and locations of duty. And above all he must be a skillful negotiator at contract time. *Fundamentals of Criminal Justice Research* facilitates the interpretation of tables, graphs, charts and symbols, the tools of contemporary bureaucratic confrontation.

Whether he faces an examination in college, an appearance before a committee or a microphone, the reader will be better prepared to deal with the complex issues. He will gain a working knowledge of the language and concepts of statistics and computers as well as an insight into the procedures and the evaluation of criminal justice research. Lucid explanations, realistic case material, and a pleasant literary style build a cushion that supports interest and understanding.

The threads of Robert Clark's varied career lines meshed to form the perfect backdrop for this book. Clark was a member of the New York City Police Department for more than twenty years, retiring with the rank of captain. As a commanding officer of a detective squad and later of a busy patrol precinct, he experienced intimately the travails of a police administrator. Although "working around the clock," he still managed to attend law school and become a member of the New York State Bar. Then continuing his graduate studies he attained the Ph.D. degree from New York University in Public Administration. For a number of years he has been a professor in the criminal justice program of Florida International University where he has specialized in teaching courses in statistics, research and methodology. If the computer has a Karma, as the author tells us in the book, then Dr. Robert Clark's Karma and destiny have prepared him uniquely to produce this work. It is a case of the right man, the right idea and the right time.

Arthur Niederhoffer
John Jay College of
Criminal Justice

Preface

This book was written for those who intend to be students of criminal justice for the major part of their professional lives. There appears to be no point at which an individual involved in criminal justice can stop studying and thinking about new approaches, new concepts, and new options. Thus the focus here is mainly on scientific ways of *thinking* about problems, and only a little bit on things to do.

That is because the things that should be done depend on the level of technology that is available at a given time and place. Technology changes so rapidly that it tends to overcome the basic importance of thinking about the what and why of a problem. Unless there is a real solution to problems of justice somewhere in the mass of figures and data, all the technology of collection and analysis will produce only a quickly fading mirage.

All modern research emerges from much the same established basic concepts. Thus a prime objective of this book is to encourage the reading of scientific research reports of all kinds with understanding, relish, and a generous dose of critical analysis. I have included actual but simplistic examples to concentrate on the *idea* of modern research without becoming embroiled in an analysis of complex issues.

I have not tried to detail all aspects of the various techniques that might be of use to research; no one text could possibly do that. Rather, I have tried to remain in a centralist position, focusing on fundamentals.

This viewpoint coincides with the position of a chief of research in a large scientific investigation, who need not have the specific and various expertises of the dozens of people whose work he coordinates. He must remain at the center, concentrating on basic issues of research design, monitoring performance, and constantly reviewing and evaluating. This person can seek expert help, of course. If he is wise, he will do so to a very great degree. But he must know to whom to go, and he must comprehend that expert's concepts and terminology.

For this reason Chapter 1 emphasizes the importance of research to modern practitioners in every field, and the fact that if they are successful in their jobs, they are already doing research. Chapter 2 offers typical applications of scientific inquiry into criminal justice, and starts with the rudiments of knowledge—what it is and how it applies to practical situations. Chapter 3 reaches farther toward providing a conceptual armament for isolating and analyzing problems. Chapter 4 explores the basic dilemmas of factual research: scaling, controlling, and auditing. Chapter 5 is a simplified review of descriptive analysis, and a practical approach for the uninitiated to understand computer printouts of descriptive statistics.

Chapter 6 reaches into inferential analysis, emphasizing concepts and applications of scientific inference to criminal justice situations and problems.

The seventh and last chapter outlines what computers can and cannot do for the average criminal justice practitioner.

The appendix, as a whole, is the how-to-do-it section of the book. It provides step-by-step guidelines for performing specific technical procedures and for resolving some current problems, such as how to quickly and easily obtain a set of descriptive statistics from a computer; how to read a research report (and by inference, how to write one); how to apply for federal funds with a reasonable hope of success; and similar nuts-and-bolts matters.

The emphasis throughout is on the concepts and terminology of science. As everyone familiar with the literature is aware, the concepts are constantly changing, accommodating to empirical discoveries and ever newer theoretical formulations. Terminology too is not uniform in the living, growing vocabulary of scientific literature. Often terms are used in various ways with differing meanings. A glossary is included to clarify the scientific usages of relevant terms.

Acknowledgments

For their sympathetic aid in all stages of preparing the manuscript, I am profoundly grateful to the entire department of mathematical sciences of Florida International University. However, I must make special mention of Professors John Comfort, Tony Berke, and Carlos Brain. I also am deeply in debt to the Southeast Regional Data Center and its staff, particularly Dr. William Wetterstrand and Betty Ruth Neilly, who have helped me over many a hurdle. I confess my gratitude to the many students who carefully read the manuscript and supplied comments that have made the book clearer and more accurate than I could have done alone. I am grateful to the Literary Executor of the late Sir Ronald A. Fisher, F.R.S., to Dr. Frank Yates, F.R.S., and to Longman Group, Ltd., London for permission to reprint tables from their book *Statistical Tables for Biological, Agricultural and Medical Research*, (6th edition, 1974). All errors and sins of omission or commission are my own doing.

**Fundamentals of Criminal
Justice Research**

1

The Professional in a World of Research

The more intelligible a thing is, the more easily it is retained in the memory, and contrariwise, the less intelligible it is, the more easily we forget it.

Spinoza
Tractatus de Intellectus Emendatione

The Modern Professional

Today's criminal justice professional is in quite a different world than even a few years ago.[1] At one time he was looked up to as an expert in his field. He knew, or was presumed to know, the world of crime and criminals and how to curb crime and violence. If he could remain impartial between contending political groups and enforce the law, dispensing punitive justice fairly and evenhandedly, his job was considered well done.[2]

Today, however, professionals are under new pressures. These forces do not so clearly reveal bias based on vested interests. The strains come from a complex technology, and from talented technologists, who arrive on the scene with many concealed assumptions inherent in their conclusions and recommendations.[3]

The modern professional must be able to comprehend and implement the welter of scientific information that comes to him daily. He must be able to read, understand, and critically evaluate research reports. He must employ a wide variety of trained analysts, such as statisticians, psychiatrists, psychologists, sociologists, and social workers. He cannot abdicate his responsibility for decision to them, however, no matter how impressive and valid their academic credentials may be. These analysts back up their advice and demands with impressive amounts of calculations and data; the practitioner must be able to weed out the valid from the invalid, taking care not to misuse the intellectual tools that have been devised to sift significant material out of the masses of information. He must not accept anything purely on faith.

Thus the individuals we need are modern professionals, specialists in their fields who can gather all the disparate elements from other fields and make

I am grateful to the editors and publishers of *The Police Chief* for permission to use the material in an article, "The Police Administrator in a World of Research," written by me, and published by them, in their December 1975 issue. Much of this material is included in the first chapter of this book.

1

judgments that will guide the social planning that has become the obligation of government at all levels. If the criminal justice professional does not understand his scientific advisers, their advice loses rational value to him, and he becomes subject to the whim of whatever technique has been funded.[4]

Decisions to fund large-scale research are not, ordinarily, his to make. Thus the findings, conclusions, and recommendations of research, and the techniques developed often come as invaders into the criminal justice agency, demanding recognition and use, without fair examination by involved practitioners.

The real decision-making power, then, goes to the technician. Until the technician or his master is charged with the responsibility for all matters of implementation, of administration, *and* of failure, we are submitting to a situation that does not lead to real progress.[5]

The complaint is not of scientific boondoggling, rather of a dilatory strategy that denies the accumulation of a body of valid knowledge in the field of criminal justice that might one day aid in opening the door to an improved society.

Not until scientific research is comprehensible to professionals and public will research find full utility and the criminal justice professional regain the right and power of decision from the mere technician.

The Professional's Task: Information Control

When the administrator's task is examined analytically, it is immediately apparent that he is occupied to a surprising extent with the problem of requesting and receiving information.

In this sense criminal justice people are astride communication centers as controllers of information.[6] For example, a police chief directs his line commanders to investigate and report; the line commander in turn directs others to collect the desired information, which is collated and sent back up the hierarchical chain. The mayor or the head of the town council may request the chief to provide information about a certain state of affairs. After obtaining the information, the chief reports back to the requesting official. At every level, information moves along established channels, and at each intersection sits a manager—though he may not think of himself as such—who directs the flow.

At each such point this information manager must examine the information with a knowing eye, make an appropriate analysis, and judge the information's validity. Sometimes he must put the data into modified form such as summaries, tabulations, or graphic representations. After his inspection, he sends the knowledge on its way, often with an indication of his own approval or disapproval. This is so, right down to the ordinary police officer at the scene of an accident.

Obviously, to exercise this type of control intelligently, these professionals require the ability to recognize the valid and the invalid.[7] They must be able to make out meanings in relation to their departments, their divisions, and their own particular assignments. They must be able to appreciate immediate consequences and ultimate effects; they must understand the strictures under which the information was collected, the purpose intended, and whether that purpose is being attained.

Allowing for specialized training in the particular tasks and problems in each position, certain generalized skills and concepts are involved in information gathering, collation, and presentation. These skills are common to both the scientific researcher and the professional in his role of controller of information.[8]

The research scientist assumes responsibility for identifying a problem and preparing a statement in form suitable to data collection, examination, and analysis. He completes his labors during presentation of all findings, explicit and implicit, in the data amassed. Usually, too, he makes recommendations regarding the implementation of various conclusions.

The close parallel with the professional's performance is obvious. Without blending professional art and experience in criminal justice with scientific discipline, both suffer.

How can these two faculties be melded? It would take far longer to train the academic researcher in the ramified reaches of criminal justice than for an experienced police or other justice official to learn to understand the language and concepts of science. They merely need to apply proper scientific terminology to much of what they have been doing.

Approaches to Knowledge

Every process in criminal justice depends on transmitted information, that is, knowledge. The information may be trivial, or of vast importance; it may be a single bit of data, or a huge mass of data. In the end, however, the entire structure of criminal justice functioning depends on knowledge that is somehow obtained, transmitted, and acted on.

Classically, methods of knowing have been summarized as authority, tradition, intuition, deductive logic, and empiricism. All these methods have been useful in the past, and are still used today.

Authority refers to matters accepted as knowledge solely on the basis of mandate. The authority can be established in an individual, a tribunal, or another source. The knowledge so obtained is often beyond verification by personal comparison with the tangible object of thought. It is so because authority has said so; discussion usually ends there.

Tradition, the accumulation of knowledge handed down from generation to generation. It often has been found serviceable in the past and no doubt it will be so in the future. However, it has often led to directly conflicting statements with no neutral guide as to what is truth or what is most in keeping with the natural world.

Intuition refers to the existence in one's mind of a certainty of something. It too has been and will continue to be useful. Its subjectivity, however, forbids any unbiased estimation of the object of thought, and it forbids verification by another person.

Deductive logic is the method of knowing that tries to follow rules of reliable inference. It too has been of great utility in obtaining useful information. Its flaw, however, is that it relies on the presumed truth of the premises of a set of arguments upon which it depends. Should any of these premises be untrue, the following arguments cannot arrive at any greater degree of truth.

Empiricism as a method of knowing relies entirely on experience. If the matter concurs with one's experience, it is considered knowledge. The potential error here is that pervasive biases are built into the method. One is that past experience very often affects present perceptions. A second is that motivation affects what we perceive as experience. A third is that memory for past experience is quite faulty. There are other flaws, not the least being that any one person's experience is necessarily limited in extent in comparison not only with all possible experience, but also in comparison with any other person's.

There is yet another method of knowing, which is not so easily subsumed as the methods cited above. This additional method, the scientific approach, tries constantly to reduce the proclivity to error of all the other methods.

The scientific approach is distinguished by a number of characteristics. First, there is a presumption that this is a real world that exists in objective, tangible form.[9] This real world is the subject of all its inquiry. This is so even when the data cannot be directly perceived by human senses, for example, radio emanations, magnetism, intelligence, and emotion. As long as an objective manifestation is available, detectable by objective means, the inquiry can be subject to the scientific approach.

Second, there is a skepticism concerning all perceptions, reasonings, and findings—in fact, this skepticism applies to every element of the scientific approach itself and even to knowing.[10]

A third attribute is that other persons must be able to replicate the knowledge.[11] That is, a detailed statement must be made of all steps taken in the inquiry so that people can be informed of exactly how the matter under investigation was studied. It is important not only that other researchers be given the information permitting them to follow all steps taken, but that such a retracing of the researcher's path actually be done by other equally qualified investigators in order to avoid subjective bias.

A fourth attribute is the provision of methods to control every conceivable source of error in the research.[12] This constant effort to avoid error permeates every part of scientific inquiry. Thus many "controls" are established. If one group of data is studied, another "control group" of data is held separate to compare with the group subjected to study, in the fear that the very act of observation has changed the nature of the data or the group in some way. Many measurements of any one phenomenon are made, with the anticipation that any of such measurements might be in error. Extreme care is used in all phases of inquiry to avoid the interjection of erroneous data either from outside the confines of the inquiry, or by the nature of the investigation itself.

A fifth attribute is the tendency to strictly limit the questions to be investigated.[13] This often results in reducing an inquiry to a single presumed relationship between two elements considered fundamental to the inquiry. This hypothesis becomes the single problem to be resolved in the scientific investigation that follows.

The hypothesis is simply a hypothetical solution to the problem of whether a suggested relationship between two elements exists. It ordinarily takes the form of a declarative sentence. An example might be, "If aggressive patrol tactics are used by a police department, the number of 'pick-up' arrests for felonies will increase." In other words, "if A then B."[14]

A of course, stands for "aggressive patrol tactics," which is postulated as an independent variable affecting the B element, or dependent-variable, which is, "arrests for felonies." The relationship suggested—"will increase"—is positive and direct. There is no imputation of agreement or belief on the part of the person posing the hypothetical relationship, just two elements and a relationship.

The hypothesis is the point of departure from which to commence the rest of the research design. It identifies the elements to be scrutinized in a form that suggests the possibility of measurement.

One can also start with a hypothetical statement that there is *no* relationship between the A and B elements, such as "If aggressive patrol tactics are used by a police department there will be no discernible effect on the number of 'pick-up' arrests for felonies."

Sometimes this "null" form of statement of the hypothesis is useful to perform certain statistical manipulations on data.[15] There is again no imputation of either belief or disbelief. It merely is another way to start the same kind of search.

The relationship in the hypothesis is stated in one direction without any suggestion that it is reversible. That is, it is hypothesized that if A is put into motion (e.g., aggressive patrol tactics are initiated), then B will ensue (e.g., there will be more, or no more, felony arrests). There is no hint that putting B into the hopper will churn out A

The variable B is presumed to be actually dependent, influenced by the *prior* existence of A, the independent variable. This defines the difference between independent and dependent variables. The dependent variable will be later in time. This fits in with most people's ideas of reasonableness: An event can influence only subsequent events. Our logic of time is that it is irreversible.

One must avoid, however, the frequently encountered fallacy of presuming that merely because an event occurred first that any subsequent event was necessarily influenced by it.

A critical point in all modern inquiry is the problem of causation. The scientific approach today does not consider ultimate causation a proper field of scientific inquiry. Instead, science pursues only the various degrees of influence that events apparently have upon each other: how the various A's affect the various B's.

Decisions regarding influence are thought to be made under uncertainty because of the random, or undetermined, situation of every A and B in the world as we know it. The scientific logic of inductive reasoning, then, is based on the notion of probability models. The "if-A-then-B" paradigm is considered merely a statement that B will occur in a certain number of cases out of a possible total number of A cases. It is a probabilistic view of the world.

Admitting honest uncertainty about estimations of the future is merely a recognition of the reality of the matter. The future is always to some degree uncertain, why not say so as exactly as possible?[16]

Research as a Simply "Open Method"

Although the scientific approach views the world as an objective entity without internal values, that does not mean it is without its own value system. The assumptions of the scientific approach listed in the previous section are, of course, value judgments. There are other values in its system, too. One such value accepted on its face is the necessity for honesty in all phases of research.

Actually, perhaps this is the most basic of all relevant assumptions. If any of the other features were to be in conflict with an open, honest view, one can expect that that characteristic or assumption would be eliminated.

Compared to some other ways of obtaining knowledge, it avoids certain characteristic traps: it makes no *a priori* decisions about the nature of the factual *elements* the observer perceives. Nor is any surmise made about the nature of the *relations* perceived or imagined to exist between those elements other than whatever is explicitly stated in the hypothesis.[17] Finally, the scientific observer makes no speculation about a predestined "order."

When order is the subject of the hypothesis itself, it is proposed only tentatively, under narrowly described conditions, with ready acknowledgment that the postulated pattern may have occurred only as a random swirl in the cosmos. There is absolutely no presumption that what is presently perceived will stand investigation for all time to come.[18]

The scientific method, then, is based on a very few assumptions, and is basically an honest, open acknowledgment of all conceivable errors in data collection and analysis. The requirement for honest candor reaches its greatest test when observations are contrary to expectations.

Likewise, it is important to set up the hypothetical relation, the "if-A-then-B" model, before obtaining any data. It would not be honest to collect data, note an interesting pattern of any given A being followed by a B, and then set up a sham research design to "prove" it.

2

Scientific Inquiry into Criminal Justice

... the outworn theory that the man is the cause of the work, as in the eyes of the law the criminal is the cause of the crime. Far rather are they both the effects.

Paul Valéry
Introduction to the Method of Leonardo da Vinci

A Typical Application: Aggressive Patrol

Alternative Hypotheses

How does the insistence on fairness and open inquiry apply in a typical situation? Take, for example, aggressive patrol tactics. Patrolmen using these tactics do not wait to observe a violation before taking action; rather, they actively stop pedestrians and auto drivers on suspicion, require them to identify themselves, and conduct preliminary investigations on the spot.

Such tactics are believed to result in frequent good arrests for felonies and misdemeanors involved in such offenses as dangerous weapons possession, narcotics, and on occasion, armed robbery. The tactics are often found objectionable, however, when innocent citizens are subjected to the delay, trouble, and inevitable harassment of such stops.

A scientific inquiry into this matter might postulate this hypothetical statement: "If aggressive patrol tactics are used by Police Department N in District 3, there will be no change in the number of 'pick-up' arrests for felonies."

An additional hypothetical statement to be examined in the same investigation could be: "Under conditions of aggressive patrol there will be no change in the attitudes of citizens regarding police."

After organized scientific research, the findings concerning these two hypotheses might be as follows:

Our findings are that a change in the number of arrests did occur. The change was positive, in the direction of the increase in aggressive patrol tactics. The change was in the proportion of about one additional "pick-up" arrest for every twenty aggressive patrol incidents. The probability that this finding is the result of chance is 5 percent.

We further find, as shown by our annexed data, that eight citizens out of ten subjected to aggressive patrol tactics felt the police action was unwarranted and oppressive. Also, the general public as revealed by a random sampling of this community appeared to change their attitudes to police in general from a scale of +5 on our attitude scale of approval to a rating of +3½. The chance that this finding is solely the result of chance is less than 5 percent according to our calculations, which are annexed.

Many police managers might think such findings are useful. Of course there are many other A's and B's that are not discussed. For example, perhaps for every twenty aggressive patrol stops (the independent variable) there were two corresponding arrests for disorderly conduct, initiated by the aggressive patrol stop itself. Or perhaps a sizable proportion of the felony arrests cited in the findings include a number of felonious assaults on the police officers involved by citizens outraged at interference with their lawful riding about town on their own business. These occurrences, had they happened, would also be relevant. In a proper inquiry they would have been subject to investigation at the same time as the two base hypotheses. These alternative hypotheses are almost always necessary in any scientific examination that is to be of maximum use to a criminal justice professional. Every imaginable A that affects people almost automatically influences unimagined, unanticipated B's. If the professional criminal justice professional does not ask these questions beforehand, who will? Because the involved researchers are deep in the facts and figures relating to aggressive patrol tactics and engrossed with completing their inquiry, it is easy for them to overlook matters such as these.

Such an "inquiry into the inquiry" is necessary before, during, and after the fact in every case. Otherwise revelation is only partial, and bias is inevitable.

This is not to imply that criminal justice professionals should perform any of the research tasks. Rather, they and members of the concerned public should provide the kind of audit and guidance that makes for an honest, open pursuit of knowledge.

Honest Knowledge About What?

Traditionally, statistics about criminal justice matters were collected for descriptive purposes. The numbers of arrests, cases closed by arrest, and so on were used to describe what the agency was doing. The number of inmates fed and housed in prison for so many days described what the correctional facility was doing. Cases disposed of by pretrial intervention described and reported on court administration and the activity of the state attorney's office. All this data collection served to satisfy the laws that required it, and it was mainly used for budgetary purposes to substantiate requests for funds.

The modern use for information, however, is to provide the basis for inferences about the processes involved in criminal justice.[1] Long experience has taught that leaps into speculation about causes of—or definitive, final solutions to—problems are invariably found wanting. Therefore inferences about relationships today omit any references to causation or to complete solution. Instead the researcher tries to develop a probability model that shows apparent relationships between independent and dependent variables.

Based on the probability model, the researcher makes inferences about probable implications. Any conclusions or decisions relying on the newly found presumed relationships are made with the distinct understanding that they are subject to further inquiry.

Whenever possible, the researcher expresses the probabilities in numerical terms, usually as percentages. Thus if A occurred 1000 times and B occurred 950 times, the probability ratio would be 950/1000, or 95 percent—that is, A "failed" to influence B in 5 percent of the possible outcomes.

The probability that the result is due to error, accident, or "random" causes can often be calculated (see Chapter 6), also as a percentage ratio. If relevant, the researcher would include a statement such as "The chance that the above finding is due to random factors is less than 1 percent." The researcher, of course, also would have to include the calculations and the data used. Without sufficient information to replicate the research *fully*, the paper is only partially representative of a scientific report.

So the answer to "Honest knowledge about what?" is "Whatever the researcher is interested in." However, what makes the knowledge honest is not the researcher's sincerity, nor true belief. The presentation must frankly admit all known biases in a form that permits anyone to estimate the probability of error.

Scientific Statements of Knowledge

As mentioned, scientific approaches to information-gathering try to build in corrective mechanisms to account for, and to correct, error. There is also a tendency to avoid concentrating on a particular problem's idiosyncracies. Rather, most researchers prefer to discover elements and relationships that are similar to whole classes of problems. This generalist approach to problem-solving has led to the formulation of many ways of thought, all of which reach for the common elements throughout many problem areas. Set thinking is one such style of viewing matters.[2]

Sets, Subsets, and Partitions

This section starts at an imagined beginning: It has been said that all human concern commences with consideration of people, and that thinking starts when one divides a subject into two classes. Dichotomization, or the thoughtful separation of a complete set of elements into two classes, is general to all human thought. A set of elements is divided along a certain dimension, or quality, as having or not having that dimension or quality. The modern computer is based on a set of switches that are turned on or off—a simple dichotomization: Electric current is divided into two mutually exclusive conditions, and there can be no other conceivable condition for the current except on or off. The entire "universe" of switches in that computer is completely partitioned into two "subsets": on switches and off switches.

Now if the entire universe of people is partitioned into men and women as two subsets that together completely encompass that entire universe, a similar partition has been made (see Figure 2-1).

This idea of a partition can be common to a host of otherwise dissimilar situations. The universe of policeman-elements can contain any number of dimensions—that is, each policeman-element has a vast number of attributes: sex, height, weight, hair color, ethnicity, nose length, intelligence, body temperature, and so on. Each one of these dimensions may be conceived as having two or more values, e.g., tall or short, heavy or light, blond or brunet or redhaired or grayhaired. There is a population of values in each dimension.

This population of values—be it a population of two, three, four, or any number of values—of a specific attribute can be partitioned. Thus the dimension of height can be viewed as consisting of a population of two values: tall and short; this population can be partitioned into tall and short as subsets that completely fill the population count, with nothing left over. The total of the subsets must exhaust the population, and they must be mutually exclusive of each other, i.e., no value or score or count can be a member of both subsets.

For more precise information, data can be collected in smaller units. Height, as an attribute, could be measured in inches, and the population of values in that attribute could be partitioned by counting all the officers who are 60 inches tall, 61 inches tall, and so on to, say, 80 inches. Subsets for officers less than 60

People

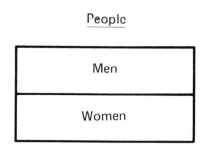

Figure 2-1. The Universe of People Divided into Men and Women.

inches and more than 80 inches would have to be included also, to exhaust all officers' heights in the population of heights. Doing so would give twenty-three subsets to partition that population.

The number of values, or scores, in each of these subsets could be counted, compared with one another, and analyzed, i.e., measured along that one dimension of height. This frequency count along the dimension of height can be called a "univariate analysis."

Crossbreaks: Bivariate Analysis

There is no reason why a universe cannot be partitioned simultaneously along more than one dimension. For example, in relation to the universe of people, the dimensions friendship and sex can be considered. These two sets of attributes can be spoken of as two different populations (P_1 and P_2) of values. Using only two values for each results in the diagram shown in Figure 2-2.

Thus the population of scores in the dimension of friendship includes the numbers in the friend and nonfriend categories. These numbers, or scores, are divided between the men and women categories in the dimension of sex. The two dimensions—P_1 and P_2—and their subsets can be diagrammed as one crossbreak. The all-inclusive set, the universe, is still people.

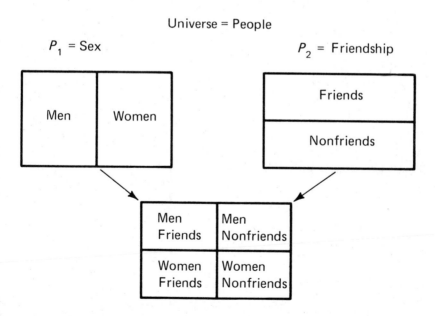

Figure 2-2. The Universe of People Partitioned into Two Populations.

One could imagine more populations of different attributes—P_1 could be divided into many more subsets, say, life-long friends, ten-year friends, one-year friends, acquaintances, and all others. Similarly, P_2 could be divided into as many subsets indicating manliness or womanliness as one could invent.

But staying with the four-box crossbreak, leaving the boxes blank, and putting the labels outside the partitioned populations gives the diagram shown in Figure 2-3. The boxes, or cells, are left blank, ready for the insertion of the appropriate numbers of the subsets.

Since the numbers in the boxes will vary from case to case, it is appropriate to call them "variables" when using the crossbreak. There are two sets, or populations, of variables, so the two-dimensional crossbreak is often called a "bivariate," or two-variable, analysis.

Filled in by a police sergeant to describe his relationship to his town, the boxes might look like the crossbreak shown in Figure 2-4.

This "2 X 2" crossbreak partition gives quite a bit of information in a very clear-cut way. It provides tabular analysis of the universe of people along two dimensions or variables, sex and friendship. The partition reveals that out of the town's total number of residents, the particular 100,000 that the sergeant has

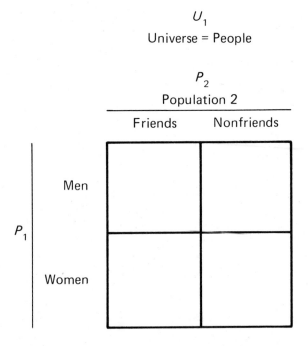

Figure 2-3. A Two-Dimensional Crossbreak.

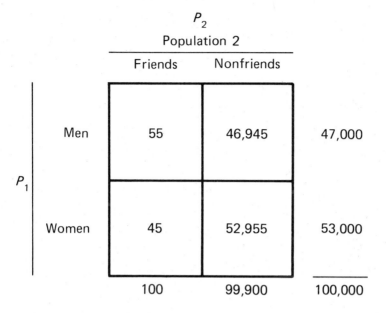

Figure 2-4. A Completed 2 × 2 Crossbreak Partition.

decided to make his "universe of discussion" can be divided along those two dimensions. The quantities, shown by the numbers, are variables, but here they are given specific values.

It is easy to perceive immediately how many male friends and how many female friends the sergeant has. The crossbreak clearly reveals the universe of discussion: the entire number of people, and how many of them are men or women. It is also easy to calculate how large a percentage of the universe are the sergeant's friends, and what percentage of his friends are men or women.

As in univariate analysis, it is essential that each dimension be mutually exclusive of the other. The word "dimension" tends to make this clear, but the term "variable," which is often used synonymously, perhaps obscures the necessity for each dimension's complete independence. Further, each dimension must be exhausted—that is, completely partitioned—with nothing left over in that dimension. However, these two dimensions do not exhaust all possible dimensions in this universe because a universe may have an infinite number of dimensions.

Multivariate Analysis

After exploring the possibilities of the bivariate analytical crossbreak, one might consider the possibility of undertaking to analyze yet another dimension of the same *universe*, say, color of hair.

One way this analysis could be diagrammed would be to construct a solid cube, adding the third dimension along the new axis. But such a diagram would be bulky and awkward. Another way would be to compare each dimension with each of the other two in pairs: A bivariate crossbreak of sex and friendship, then another of sex and color of hair, and finally another of friendship and color of hair. The three sets of crossbreaks together would show all possible combinations of relations.

Still another way of diagramming is shown in Figure 2-5. Each of the three dimensions is split into two subsets, giving an abundance of information. This diagram is called a $2 \times 2 \times 2$ crossbreak; each digit represents a different dimension is involved; the "2's" indicate that each dimension is split into *two* subsets.

Admittedly, the diagram is getting a bit complicated. There is, however, no theoretical reason why a researcher could not make a four-dimensional crossbreak with dichotomized subsets—a $2 \times 2 \times 2 \times 2$ crossbreak—or even a five-variable crossbreak with dichotomized subsets—a $2 \times 2 \times 2 \times 2 \times 2$ crossbreak. Interpretation would tend to become confused in these multidimensional tables. In practice, a three- or four-variable crossbreak is about the upper limit.

Instead of merely dichotomizing each dimension (splitting each into two subsets), a researcher could divide each dimension into three, four, or even more parts. A 5×5 crossbreak, or even a 10×10 crossbreak is quite possible. Thus even though the researcher retains only a two-dimensional crossbreak, he might

P_3 = Hair Color

		Blond		Nonblond		
		P_2 = Friendship		P_2 = Friendship		
		Friends	Nonfriends	Friends	Nonfriends	
P_1	Men	20	20,000	35	26,945	47,00
	Women	40	20,000	5	32,955	53,00
		60	40,000	40	59,900	100,00

Figure 2-5. A Three-Dimensional, or Three-Variable, Crossbreak.

increase the information presented by increasing the number of parts into which a given dimension is subdivided. For example, here are ten possible subsets for each of the two variables friendship and color of hair.

Friendship	Color of hair
Life-long friend	Black
Very good friend	Dark brown
Friend	Light brown
On friendly terms	Blond
Acquaintance	Auburn
Hardly know person's name	Red
Recognize, but don't know	Iron-gray
Don't recognize	All gray
Don't think ever saw person	White
Complete stranger and all others	Bald and all others

It would be easy to tabulate ten values, or subsets, of one of these variables on ordinary typing paper if that variable were placed along the vertical axis of the paper. It would be inconvenient, however, to have ten subdivisions (subsets) strung all along the top of an extremely wide sheet of paper. For that reason crossbreaks may have many values in one variable, but rarely will they have too many along the other dimension in a two-dimensional crossbreak. When three dimensions are involved, it is almost always convenient to have very many subdivisions of only one of them.

Despite the complications in the presentation of information involving multivariate analysis, the current trend in research is to reach for as many variables as are both relevant and convenient, because there are many variables, known and unknown, that are involved in almost any real-life situation or criminal justice program.

In any event, it should be clear why scientific statements need not be in ordinary English. Even phrases such as "exhaustive and mutually exclusive" can be shown in diagrammatic form by the crossbreak, and the diagram can convey information in a form that would be practically impossible to comprehend in English sentences. Even more information could be displayed by the $2 \times 2 \times 2$ crossbreak if the relative percentages were included in each cell. A computer can do so automatically (see Figure 5-5).

Variables: Categorical and Continuous

After specific individuals are assigned to the various subsets, they can be thought of in an organized way so that a researcher clearly understands which attribute of each individual is being discussed, and which relationship is the one with which he is concerned.

The two subsets men and women are independent of each other, and they are "categorical" in that there is an assumption that each is discrete—there is no subset between them.

Most people have no trouble thinking of these two subsets as categorical. But considering such subsets as all the men's and women's heights, or weights, or degrees of skill is more difficult, because those variables are continuous, that is, there are no natural breaks that make categories obvious. This situation was somewhat evident in the dimension color of hair, which included arbitrary categories of colors with names and places in the scheme with the presumption that the list was "exhaustive and mutually exclusive."

Ordinarily there is no imputation of relative value in categorical subsets. However, when a researcher arbitrarily categorizes valued continuous relationships such as height, weight, and length, this is not so.

Specifically, men and women, as partition-subsets of a universe of all people, have no relative value relationship. Nor do apples, oranges, pears, and "all other" fruits, as a four-variable-subset of the universe of fruits, have any value relationship among them. But if a researcher categorizes all patrolmen's heights, as a universe, into the two mutually exclusive and exhaustive categories short and tall, he does *not* eliminate the intrinsic quantitative relationship between them.

Such arbitrary categorization of continuous variables causes a researcher to lose information: the specific details revealed in the continuous (or nearly so) measures of height. That loss is necessary, however, if the information is to be expressed in a crossbreak; if algebra were used, continuous measures might be possible because the language of algebra is better adapted to describing continuous variables.

Usually, however, not too much is lost by categorization: the very act of practical measurement forces some degree of categorization. While measurement need not be so coarse as to class all patrolmen over, say, 5 feet, 10 inches as tall, and all others as short, in any real-life situation measurements of human height to degrees smaller than ¼ inch are rather fatuous. The average young man may change in height during the course of a day by as much as ½ inch or more.

Even a computer cannot use continuous measurement data to a finer degree than its physical construction and programming permits. The ten or more significant digits in its output necessarily categorize the numerical values fed into it, even though the number of such categories can number in the billions.

The language of partitioning and crossbreaks, however, can provide for only a very limited number of categories. Tabular presentations reach a practical upper limit in reference books of tabled numerical values for mathematical functions such as logarithms. The upper limit is decided simply by convenience. This rule of convenience holds most graphed data presentations to between seven and twenty categories along either axis. Thus higher mathematical methods for multivariate analysis have been developed in the attempt to expedite the complexities involved. In practical research, however, even these methods have seen limited application.

In any case the relationships between pairs of variables such as patrolmen's intelligence scores and their success or failure as personnel; their weight and the time lost for illness; and countless other bivariate relationships are of intense interest to managers, and they are easily collected and displayed in tabular or graphic form.

Elements

Elements in the previously cited universes were identified as units, either categorical items or values of a certain population of such units or values within a specific dimension.

In univariate analysis, the numbers that measure the amount of each element that "go with" each other *element* are counted; the police sergeant had 100 friends of whom 45 were women. In bivariate analysis, the elements (of one population along a certain dimension) "go with" specific elements of another population along another dimension.

The *elements* considered earlier varied from men and women to felony arrests and accident rates. The elements could, in fact, be anything, as long as they are identifiably of the same subset. The list of possible elements is, of course, endless.

Relationships as "Ordered Pairs"

It is easy to imagine that relations between elements could be in a spatial dimension such as inside or outside. Including a linear component can produce such relations as over, under, behind, alongside, and so on. In a time dimension, there are such relationships as sooner than, later than, before, and after.

In trying to find a more general definition of relations than to recite such specific terms as above, dictionaries have used words such as "bond" and "connection." A phrase that seems to offer even more usefulness as a definition of relationship is "ordered pairs"—"ordered" means whatever "order" may be designated; the "pairs" are any two elements whatever.[3]

The usefulness of the ordered pairs definition was evident from the previous matching of man with his corresponding paired state of being a friend, all through the list of such man-friends, then with woman and woman-friends. Then each such pair—now being considered an element—was paired with its corresponding blond-element. Although three dimensions were analyzed with three separate populations of categories, the analysis was actually reduced to the comparison of ordered pairs.

A crossbreak shows ordered pairs in tabular form at each intersection. These ordered pairs are—or can be reasonably considered—categorical. When the categories come naturally out of the data, there is no problem, but some information is lost when categories are forced on the data. Whether the data should be handled as categorical or continuous is often a matter of balancing convenience against accuracy.

Finally, it will be very helpful to remember a definition of knowledge as consisting simply of "conclusions about relations"—or, in the general form that has been found almost universally useful, "if A then B."

The A and B relationship, as stated, is an ordered pair; usually there are a great number of ordered pairs: sets and subsets. If the A's and B's are known, they can be listed in a bivariate table, graph, or other representation. If they are unknown, they can be sought by a research procedure and thereafter listed. If they can be best expressed as a proposition, or a "rule of correspondence," between them, perhaps the best method of presentation would be to state the rule of correspondence: If A is any given number, add two to get B.

Useful Patterns of Relations

The previous section noted that the general form "if A then B" expresses a notion of correspondence between sets of ordered pairs of elements. This is a general proposition—more general than one imputing influence by A on B. It permits, however, the use of the if-A-then-B model to represent virtually any hypothetical statement of influence or mere correspondence. Correspondence can be observed; influence, however, is a leap into speculation. No matter how certain one may be of alleged influence, it is not quite a probability of 1, or certainty.

Therefore scientific research observes only correspondence and restricts its data and findings to keeping a record of such correspondences. The imputation of influence is properly left to conclusions, which are stated, preferably in ratio form.[4]

Not all imagined or observed patterns of if A then B correspondences are of equal interest. The criminal justice professional is interested only in patterns that offer hope of being useful. Although there are infinitely many conceivable relationships, most researchers are interested only in a small subset of them.

Determining the subset of "research-worthy" relationships is a task calling for value judgments mainly beyond the reach of objective ascertainment. Here again the experienced criminal justice practitioner provides a resource essential to the production of dollar-efficient inquiry. What professional has not wondered about the real relationships among the myriad facts and factors he deals with in a working day? Would spending more money on equipment save salary costs? Would spending more time on community relations reduce the likelihood of crisis situations in a given area?[5]

It is true that an outside research expert coming with a fresh insight may pick up on an interesting or important relationship that calls for inquiry. Generally, however, the practitioner has as many questions as answers. The questions that bother practitioners are the ones that cry for answers loudest, for they could solve urgent present problems.

Immediate Needs

Most of the criminal justice professional's time is spent trying to solve the immediate problems that beset him. He rarely has the time or inclination to analyze a given problem for elements common to problems in general, for much of his activity is in response to crisis.[6]

Active "firefighting" such as is found in criminal justice reactions to critical situations is not conducive to the calm, reflective analysis that would tend to accumulate organized information and programs that would effectively prevent the recurrence of emergencies.

The professional's entire training has been to cut through deadwood to get to the heart of the matter as it has been seen in traditional forms. Now that traditional techniques are being reexamined and new decisions being called for, it is important not to forget that the emergency nature of criminal justice decisions has not been removed. There may be ways to prevent prison riots, there may be ways to prevent the catastrophic consequences of such riots. Researcher and practitioner are actively seeking the means for such prevention. But until they come up with verified solutions and procedures, there seems to be no acceptable way to avoid the personal and community disasters associated with criminal justice performance.

It is because the practitioner is preoccupied with his daily task of crisis intervention that help should and can be sought from the realm of science.[7]

Adding to Knowledge–the Object of Science

The criminal justice professional makes many decisions by rule of thumb, by an informal estimation of likelihood of success, and with many undefined elements and relationships implicit in the process of his decision-making, but this may not be a matter of choice. Much of the data on which decisions are based are relevant only to the current situation. Slowly, perhaps, experience may expose many similar situations, and a more certain way of handling typical issues may emerge. Unfortunately, much of that knowledge remains private to the individual, and little goes into a storehouse of knowledge that is available to others. Admittedly, some small amount becomes common property, in the form of rules that are formally drawn up, procedures and techniques. But the professional's main objective is to solve his problems of the day.

The scientist's purpose, however, is to accumulate knowledge and record it so that others may read it and use it.[8] Thus the scientist reaches for objectivity with a passion. In the real world the route toward objectivity is through methods and data that others can duplicate independently. A standard auditing principle is followed: cut the connections of interested parties. Self-interest tends to warp perceptions.

A number of accepted rules or procedures have been developed to cut those connections. They are not strict in form, but they are rigorous in their objective: to reduce the probability of error. The process involves efforts to reduce extraneous variables, to discover error when it creeps in, and constantly to trace through the research to find flaws.

Some of the specific research recommendations are:

1. Keep a diary of every relevant act in connection with the research. Include, if possible, every line of thought, so that later review will recall on-scene perceptions.
2. Include in the diary the reason for every decision, so that each can be reassessed later.
3. After a preliminary survey of the problem area, prepare the hypotheses that will be subjected to inquiry. Avoid formulating hypotheses merely on the basis of observed patterns in the preliminary survey, which may be the result of random or accidental influences unless due care is taken to avoid error.
4. Carefully set up a research design to control or eliminate potential errors and accidents. Outline in the research design the conditions under which all data will be collected, the kinds of data, and the methods of reporting the data to the researcher.
5. Employ qualified expert analysts, statisticians, and computer specialists to verify the appropriateness of the form in which it is proposed to collect and to present the data for analysis, and to be sure the analytical methods proposed are the best for the problems presented. Carefully examine all assumptions implicit in data form and analytical method, as well as instrumentation used.
6. Supervise data collection to ascertain that all requirements of the research design are met.
7. Frequently review all procedures and concepts during the course of the research.
8. Under no circumstances alter any data, however out of line they may appear, without sufficient justification. Record that fact in the diary and in other records.
9. Preferably have noninterested parties collect data—best of all is machine-collection—to reduce bias.
10. Have noninterested parties summarize and analyze data for findings.

11. Carefully separate speculative conclusions and recommendations from the objective data and findings in the final report. Even if no relationship is found between the A's and the B's of the hypothesis, that is knowledge, and it should be so treated.

The Professional's Obligations

The professional's obligations all revolve around his organizational objectives.[9] Insofar as they apply to scientific research, the following matters should be of major concern in his endeavor to meet research principles halfway:[10]

1. To perceive all relevant aspects of problems and issues in analytical form—that is, to try to reduce them to elements and relationships;
2. To identify and understand these elements and relationships by objective means—that is, to isolate value judgments;
3. To apply all discovered knowledge to the reach for his organizational goals;
4. To aid in the accumulation of a body of valid, rational knowledge in criminal justice.

It appears that circumstance thrusts these obligations on the criminal justice professional, but actually, the continuing search for useful patterns of relations is as much a part of his job as his paycheck. He cannot take refuge in older patterns without recourse to the kind of conceptual justification that itself constitutes a search for useful patterns of relationships.

This is not to mean that analyzing all problems into elements and relationships will automatically produce a one-on-one instant comparison and solution of competing problems. Rather, the effort will tend to clarify the issues, put problems in proportion, and—perhaps most important—enable the practitioner to communicate the essence of his thoughts to others who can more objectively assist in analysis and comprehension. Not until the researcher attains this coordination of intelligences will he obtain the kind of monitoring and evaluative feedback that will keep him on course.

The Generalist View

The professional manager is charged with overall responsibility for results.[11] As such, he is charged, as a "generalist," to balance the efforts of all.

It is rare to find an academic researcher who does not have a specific area of specialty, whether it be social work, sociology, psychology, political science, education, or something else. Together with that occupational bias, a research director will bring his own personal predilections and prejudices, as any other person would.

In view of the vast need for research and the great dependence that practitioners will have on research in the future, and in consideration of the huge sums involved and wide public interests, there seems to be a need to refresh concern for a centralist position.

The center position is perhaps best summarized by a review of the acknowledged goals of a criminal justice agency. These goals are often stated in enabling laws, policy statements issued by top management or accumulated in a series of statutes or other public acts. A group of people at each level is charged with the responsibility for accomplishing these lawful, acceptable goals. These people are responsible for making decisions based on their personal understanding and discretion. Sometimes these professionals have the task of evaluating entire programs, which is necessary for internal decisions about whether the program is attaining its goals and thus whether it deserves continued effort. There are also many persons outside the organization to be satisfied. It is up to these information managers to provide the evidence.

Here is where few could deny that the language of science and research is the only speech that will be acceptable to the public and its representatives. They want *fact* they can believe in, not authority, tradition, intuition, nor even simplistic empiricism.

Figure 2-6 is a diagrammatic picture of the problems and variables. Note the resemblance to the basic if-*A*-then-*B* model. The *A* here is the program. The program introduces the *A* variable into a situation, as a "treatment." The *B* is the effect, the dependent variable, or the result expected from the treatment.

There is added, however, recognition that a vast number of other variables existed before, during, and after the program. These variables very possibly acted on the same subject elements the program (the independent variable) affected.

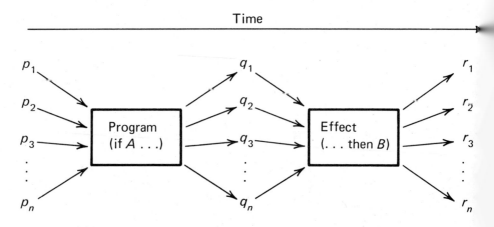

Figure 2-6. Diagram of the Problems and Variables.

The horizontal axis represents the time dimension, and the p's indicate the variables of unknown number and character that acted on the subject elements before the program started. The q's stand for the variables, not knowingly in the program, that acted during the program's existence and before the effect was expected. The r's stand for the variables that affect the subject elements after the effect was measured, possibly changing those elements. In each case the subscripts merely show that there is an unknown number of each of these extraneous variables.

What the chief of a program wants is to maximize the effect of the program—to get the most B for the A that is applied.

A program almost certainly provides a number of different inputs, or A variables, that are applied to subject-elements. These A's could have been marked $A_1, A_2, A_3, \ldots, A_n$ to show that the program supplies a number of different identifiable treatments. For example, a program to reduce crime may be designed to include changing patrol hours, different procedures established, and media presentations designed to enlist citizen cooperation—all as parts of the program treatment, or A variable. Likewise the dependent variable sought, the effect, may have been a reduced number of robberies, or increased public satisfaction, symbolized $B_1, B_2, B_3, \ldots, B_n$.[12]

A different program, aiming at the effect of rehabilitating prison inmates can be analyzed in similar fashion: the researcher knows the effect, the B variable, because he defines what he wants himself. He chooses, say, a reduced rate of return to jail—a reduced recidivism rate—as the measure of rehabilitation.

Then he devises a treatment (A variable) to apply. Suppose he sets up a point system of credits earned for passing vocational skills tests, hoping that those who become proficient in salable skills would be more likely to find jobs on release and therefore would be less likely to commit crimes, be caught, and thus returned to prison.

Then the researcher makes vocational skill training available to the inmates, and thereafter tests his subjects for skills attained. From that point in this continuing program, he keeps track of former students and testees to obtain figures concerning the frequency at which they are returned to prison. If the rate is much less—say, 10 percent less—than the return rate of those who did not go to school or attain high grades on the tests, can he say the program is succeeding?

Most people connected with such a program would say that the program is outstandingly successful, but the success is *not* really proved. So many extraneous variables are involved that might have been more influential than A and have not been accounted for.

Considering the p's, the variables occurring before the treatment, the researcher should ask, What was the effect of the p called "selective factors"? That is, what was the process of determining the prisoners' eligibility for vocational training? Were some inmates excluded? Were those that were excluded just those that would be likely to be recidivists? If so, the researcher left out a portion of the group that requires representation if he is interested in the effect of vocational skill training on recidivism.

There are many other p's that a little creative imagination, or inquiry, can list, such as inmates' perception of the relevance of the training to themselves and their future; the inmates' cultural backgrounds; the ambience of the prison institution; other alternatives available to inmates; and so on.

Considering q's, the researcher should ask, Did all inmates receive the same training in the same modes or styles? Were some teachers "better" than others? Did food, rest, or time off vary for some inmates?

Considering r's, the researcher should ask, Has the program been in effect long enough to have an effect on the recidivist rate? Are jobs more available now than last year? Have some ex-inmates moved out of the state, so that figures for them are unavailable? Many other r's may come to his mind.

It is easy to think a program effective when all variables have not been considered. For example, the governor of Connecticut, after a one-year program of strict traffic-law enforcement, announced on the basis of accident figures unequivocal confidence that the lowered accident rate "proved" the program's success, but subsequent years' figures did not substantiate that claim. One should not have so high a stake in the result that one's judgment is biased.

This full-dimensional approach to problem-solving is multivariate analysis. That there are multiple variables in real-life situations is common knowledge, but identifying them, measuring them, and balancing them calls for the most adroit management skills and clear-headed analysis.

The alien variables p, q, and r must be minimized, especially insofar as they tend to mitigate the effect; they are "errors."

The generalist goals are to get the job done, to obtain the desired effect, to attain the major goals of the program, if possible. But in any case he tries to understand what influences operated.[13]

Investigation is not new to the criminal justice professional—it is the stuff of his occupational life. With the commitment that criminal justice demands, many in the field live and breathe investigation almost every waking hour. The basic concepts of good investigation and fair inquiry are well within their ability.

Science, however, uses many languages not immediately comprehensible to the practitioner. This language problem consists mainly in the use of ordinary words in special ways, certain rules in graphic presentations, and certain relationships that occasionally call for complex statements to be precise. If the statements are very complex, often the most convenient way to express them in compact form is symbolically.

All this, however, is really not very much of an obstacle to comprehension at the desired operational level required of the modern criminal justice professional. He is accustomed to using interpreters in his investigations and in other aspects of his work. True, it is useful to be able to catch the meaning of an ongoing translation lest the entire thrust of translated questions and answers go the wrong way. But the professional need not become highly proficient in the various scientific jargons. His function is to keep the path of the research conceptually true to valid operational goals, and in this manner to aid in building a real science of criminal justice.[14]

Program Evaluation

Program evaluation is the "bottom line" in administration. Thousands of program evaluations have been written, most of them quite self-serving, and understandably so.[15] The continuance of a program, its funding, and the very professional life of an administrator may hinge on a program's favorable evaluation.

The recent trend has been to try to include program evaluation as an intrinsic continuing part of the program; the object is to receive continuous feedback during the program's term in order to avoid any major errors. As a part of this there has been an increasing reach for "outside evaluators" who are less involved in the program's fate, and therefore perhaps less biased and more nearly approaching audit principles.

A constant concern in evaluation is the detection of unanticipated consequences and their appropriate measurement and weighting,[16] which may be the best reason to use disinterested evaluators. It is difficult for a researcher, deeply involved with his work, to discover at the end of his program entirely different dimensions than those with which he has been so profoundly concerned. They tend to remain beyond his ken.

If a program was designed not merely for its own sake but to attain an identifiable objective, certainly all well-intentioned efforts to determine to what extent that objective has been attained are good. In addition, there are a great number of other useful results from proper evaluation, ranging from the discovery of new *B*'s and new dimensions of concern, building morale in a goal-seeking sense, to system-building toward a more coherent criminal justice structure.

Thus it is just as important to identify evaluation objectives as it is to identify program objectives. Unless these objectives are separately identified and clear statements made, the conflicts and role relationships between practitioner and evaluator become intolerable. These issues become most poignant when short-term and long-term objectives are intermingled without distinction.

These are only some of the reasons for the conspicuous failure of evaluation research to attain the degree of success hoped for it. The greatest conflicts will arise when the evaluator challenges the basic concepts of the program. But if the evaluator does not do so, the most important area of evaluation will have been ignored. It is only when basic concepts are reviewed in light of present conditions that evaluation can really influence programs and all administrative action. And if evaluation is not to influence action, why have it at all?

3

Research Design

Many things difficult to design prove easy to performance.

Samuel Johnson
Rasselas, Chap. I

The title of this book promises guidelines for professionals as generalists in a world of research. This role is conceived as that of participant-critic and judge. The credentials required are familiarity with criminal justice policies, practices, and procedures, plus a liberal dash of judicial temperament.

This broad view of research calls for a design that accepts the necessity for experts, as technicians, in a dozen fields in any large-scale inquiry. Even smaller research projects often have manifold aspects that require at least occasional consultation with specialists in specific disciplines.

Thus the criminal justice professional is constantly faced with problems that must be resolved on the basis of efforts and resolutions for which he is responsible. Decision-making then, should be removed from the technician, whatever his expertise.

It may not go as far as the statement that "Technicians are just a figment of the chief's imagination; the chief gets all the credit, so he should get all the blame." The general tone, however, is correct. The professional who is responsible for results should remain in control of information and research implementation.

Research—for What?

The criminal justice professional, in this perspective, becomes a part of the research team at the very inception of the inquiry, when the first questions are asked: Is there a problem, and what is it?

The professional may not see a problem that appears quite clear to a layman. Problems of agency impact on the community often are of that nature. A community or a portion of a community will declare the existence of a problem sometimes long before the governmental agency involved will be able to focus on it clearly.

In that sense, often it has seemed that ameliorative change comes only from the outside, but that is not the whole story. Although clientele notice a problem

29

first, the agency itself, if not brought into the matter promptly, tends to remain permanently estranged, and the implementation of even the most desirable change will be faced with massive inertia. This is without even considering that there is a low likelihood of discovering a viable solution without the agency's active participation.

If, on the other hand, the criminal justice professional is brought into the matter immediately to aid in resolving the problem, the stage will have been set for the participation that encourages sophisticated inquiry and successful implementation. This implementation starts with research design.

Research design is the tactical plan of the research. It sets up a framework of adequate tests of relations among the variables. It will often cite what observations of data will be made, and how. It may even dictate the number of observations that will be made, the way the observation will be performed, and the training of the observers. It will specifically state the hypotheses to be tested, the tests to be used, and the time schedule for the research.

Further, the research design will outline in detail the proposed analyses of all collected information, with specific proposals of quantitative representations, summaries, and indexes that are planned to be used, in the presentation of results.

A research design that is prepared *after* the fact is worse than useless. It inevitably, and fraudulently, reaches to conceal embarrassing preconceptions and fundamental errors. It is the antithesis of honest, open scientific inquiry.[1]

A research is successful if the process of scientific inquiry is kept inviolate. That is the full measure of the inquiry's validity. *A priori* decisions regarding desired conclusions have no fair part. Such objectives may be necessary to a manager, but biased unscientific investigation is not the way to attain them. A true professional reaches for impartiality with a passion.

Purpose and Its Implications

Often the proposed research announces its purpose by its very terms. "What's a better way to handle domestic disturbances?" Or "How can prison inmates be rehabilitated on release?"[2]

It is not enough, however, to let the matter lie there. Invariably, examination will reveal more purposes than those stated. It is useful to try to determine all possible purposes, stated and unstated, and to rate them as to their relevancy to the administrator's general goals and to the goals of the proposed research.

If the basic aim is to provide quick answers to a crisis situation, it is expected that approach and method may well be different from an inquiry that has as its objective internal determination of relative values and malfunctions of a proposed new procedure. If the purpose is to obtain factual substantiation for a budget request, another set of decisions about time, money, and effort will be made.

A crisis—such as the sudden discovery in the spring that a violent summer is in the offing due to a rise in unemployment and increased agitation and disorganization in poverty-stricken sections of a large city—may call for large amounts of personnel over a short period.

Other cases may mandate a more dilatory strategy. Thus the problem in reading reports or proposals of research involves some perceptive reading-in of motives and tradeoffs.

To obtain skill in perceiving the subliminal hints of purpose barely indicated in the reports, it is helpful to prepare proposals, work in research projects, and join in the collation and reduction of findings and conclusions into completed research reports. Doing research proposals, projects, and reports is the way to learn what they are all about.

Isolating Problem Areas

Usually a problem in criminal justice will present different aspects to the examiner. One set might revolve about administration, internal and external relations with other agencies, or relations with community. Another set might concern impacts on personnel as affecting work habits, prestige relationships, or salary differentials. There are so many other conceivable angles from which any given problem can be viewed that it would be impossible to make any list of reasonable size that would have probable relevance to a specific problem.

Generally, however, a problem can be divided into pieces. The important segments often range in a continuum, from the comparatively known to the unknown. This has led to a general rule: Usually it is more productive to work from the known to the unknown, isolating the critical problem areas from the noncritical. The key to simplification is to isolate problem-areas into a series of if-*A*-then-*B* statements.

After such analysis is well on its way but before it is completed, it is frequently useful to step back and review the entire situation. Often the problem has taken on a new shading after some detailed exploration of subareas. A heuristic furthering of discovery of new facets is the objective, even toward "solutions" that one is quite sure will not work.

Often the brainstorm that uncovers a previously overlooked "if-*A*-then-*B*" has a facility for making desirable but unsought discoveries. Many a serendipitous hypothesis will make its belated appearance only after an exhausting, exasperating rehash of almost-forgotten, long-discarded ideas.

Design—for What?

Research design aims to (1) bring evidence to bear on if-*A*-then-*B* questions, and (2) control error.

Decisions concerning the nature of the evidence to be collected should be made prior to actually proceeding with the research; otherwise it will become well nigh impossible to formalize the data collection procedure sufficiently to design in the safeguards necessary to avoid contaminating data with extraneous factors. A grab bag of evidence of all kinds, without discipline or standards of collection methods, inevitably becomes disorderly in detail and chaotic in presentation.

The researcher is interested in isolating the subject of inquiry as much as is practical from influence other than the selected A's. He also wants to note clearly all consequent B's.

The presence of influences other than A diffuse A's effect. The presence of conditions other than B obscure the observation of B.

A researcher cannot ordinarily attain a truly laboratory situation with all irrelevant variables sedulously excluded, although that would be ideal. Insofar as he approaches this truly experimental mode, he validates his research design. He settles for much less even though he tries for more.

Every detail of a planned research must be perused beforehand to eliminate such unwarranted errors as variation in measurements of treatments. Careful pretest evaluations must be planned. It is essential to prepare and assign control groups that will not be treated, in order to determine whether it is possible to observe B without prior application of A. All data relevant to the if-A-then-B model should be as free from error and bias as possible. In sum, it is vital to have *all admissible evidence*.

The evidence that is wanted concerns variables, and other planned-for data. The unwanted matter includes all stray influences on the pattern of A's and B's that fog the issues. In the aggressive patrol example, variations in the *style* of the officers involved might be such an unwanted variable. Some officers might "come on" in a low-key, gentle manner and voice. Others might habitually use violent language and gestures, without otherwise performing differently in aggressive patrol evolutions. This unwanted variable, style, might interfere with any findings about the specific if-A-then-B relationships being investigated. To avoid such an undesired variable, a standardized approach and presentation could be designed into the experiment: for example, a schedule of approach and presentation of requests to be made of the members of the public in the field situation.

From the research point of view, there may be no requirement that a policeman's style be either high-key or low-key. The important thing would be to standardize the style as much as possible so that it would not throw off the comparison of results of different police teams as evidence is collected for the research project.

"Variance control" includes organized effort to maximize the variance of A and B so that any relationship between them will be easily observed, and if possible, measured. That is, the design will be set up where, as, and how the clearest pattern of A's and B's can be anticipated.

In the aggressive patrol example, the research design would not undertake to find patterns of aggressive patrol, and consequences such as felony arrests and civilian complaints, under a research design that would not contemplate the ease or difficulty of receipt of civilian complaints. If all civilian complaints were not accepted as data unless presented in a strictly formal manner, at a specific location, within a certain time limit, one can imagine that they would tend to drop out of the pattern of A's and B's. In short, means must be provided for collecting all available data about A's and B's as part of variance control.

There is yet another part of variance control: the effort to control the variance of unwanted variables. Thus variance control envisages all efforts to minimize random variance, including errors of measurement. An example of this kind of variance would be the irregular reporting of aggressive patrol "incidents" caused by a lack of standards to identify aggressive situations from other variations of patrol. The potential for error is always high in reporting methods that depend on human discretion, which is why the research community has suggested that all effort be made to use mechanical methods for reporting data.

People with vested interests in events cannot be permitted to report on them with even a remote hope that errors will cancel each other out. A vested interest acts as a systematic bias; even if the population being sampled is very large, systematic errors will not cancel out and the bias will remain.

Even when human discretion is not viewed as tending toward systematic bias, such randomly erroneous complexes of variance are weak ground for founding scientific results. Skepticism, "detective methods," and avoidance of what insurance companies call "moral risk" must be the watchwords in this entire area. There is enough unavoidable error without courting unnecessary hazard.

With all these caveats regarding error—and perhaps a new feeling for sources of variance—the aggressive patrol example can be evaluated *in toto* for potential error.

It is now quite clear that allegedly "researching" aggressive patrol techniques, reporting them, and counting felony arrests and civilian complaints constitute an intrinsically error-filled approach with many occasions for extraneous variance. The gaps in careful design are numerous: any changes noted in the number of arrests could be caused by factors other than the independent variable. Some of these intrusive factors might be: policemen's increased interest in the assignment as an elite one; an otherwise unnoticed increase in criminal possession of firearms due to an influx of such guns from outside the city; or conditions of domestic unrest that encourage citizens to be armed with guns while riding in their autos.

One way to try to avoid these sources of error in the research design would be to provide a "control group" that was *not* subjected to aggressive patrol. The control group, or control area, would provide figures that could be compared with those of the experimental area being "treated," to determine if a similar change in B has occurred without the benefit of the treatment.

After a predetermined time, the control area could change roles and become the experimental area—the former control area would then be aggressively patrolled, with appropriate reporting of all relevant events, and the former experimental area would then be routinely patrolled. Another control that could be established would be to use the same, or different, patrol teams, to try to eliminate sources of error arising in team behavioral characteristics, familiarity with the area, and other idiosyncratic aspects of the personnel.

At this early point in considering possible research designs for this project, it would seem that several control, experimental, and other areas should be considered, as well as a highly structured plan for the placement and replacement of policemen assigned. The effort to control variance inevitably leads to multigroup designs.

One-group designs, such as the experiment on aggressive patrol as originally proposed, are considered scientifically worthless because they tend to misinform. This is so whether the one-group design is devoted to collecting evidence empirically, or collecting it ex post facto, in the sense that all data was amassed previously and the research involves merely an analysis of existing police records.

It is unforgivable to use such weak research designs, which fail for lack of realization of their inherent flaws.

One must admit, however, that although one-group and other faulty research designs always leave room for the entry of unwanted variance, they have often been consciously used as a matter of convenience or economy of resources. In such cases the practitioner is concerned with results he can use, not the niceties of research procedure. Nevertheless, he must be aware of possible sources of error so he can reasonably evaluate findings and conclusions and know the grounds to defend or abandon policies founded on them.

Many quite complex research designs have been developed, with multiple control and experimental groups and randomly assigned treatments, all in the effort to exclude extraneous variance and thus minimize the risk of error. A large body of literature has developed dealing with such designs.[3] It would be valuable to the criminal justice professional to compare the ideal designs suggested in these texts with the research design proposed to provide him with "scientific managerial data." He would then be in a much better position to evaluate the findings and conclusions of such research.

Data Sources

When the problem area has been thoroughly explored, the various hypotheses formally recorded, and the outline of the research design at least tentatively discussed, the time has come to set up specific procedures arranged to determine whether the *A*'s affect the *B*'s, that is, to test the hypotheses. But first the researcher must outline the data sources.

Often criminal justice problems have been worked and reworked countless times in distant places, without a given police department or correctional institution's being aware that the problem has been solved or at least that some facets of the solution have been revealed. To avoid the profitless waste of doing again what may have been done before, the researcher should carefully review the literature. Documentary research is a specialty in itself that calls not only for particular knowledge of places where relevant information is stored, but also for skill in retrieving that information.

Every good library gives an extended listing of bibliographic data sources that apply in some degree to almost any imaginable problem. Additional resources should also be compiled. A careful, searching inquiry in every direction is important not only to uncover actual, relevant data, but also to acquaint others with the search so they are less resistant to findings or even conclusions when they finally appear.

When a fair amount of library or historical data has been assembled and reviewed, the researcher should ask what, if any, additional data should be developed out of the current inquiry: What empirical approach? The researcher must more specifically outline various possible practical operational measures of the B's, the criteria that are expected. If these attributes are easily counted, there should be no serious problem. Such an attribute might be the number of applicants for the position of patrolman, or corrections officer. The criterion measure of B is easily measured itself, by counting the applications on file before and after the treatment.

On the other hand, some B's are much more difficult to estimate accurately. For instance, "good public relations with the community," as a dependent criterion value, is an imponderable reality that is not measurable to everyone's satisfaction.

In such a case an arbitrary decision must be made to accept a specific procedure as a measure—making such a decision and acting on it is called "operationalization." The researcher hopes that the majority of interested parties can be induced to accept the measure chosen: an opinion survey, a sampling of the community, a reduced count of civilian complaints, an increase in favorable editorial comments in the local newspaper, or whatever.

A researcher can devise operational measures by the dozens. The choice ultimately will be the most convenient, possibly after a preliminary test to determine applicability, and after a comparison of the various operational measures' difficulty of accomplishment with their acceptability as valid measures.

In all these cases, however, the researcher will seek empirical facts, which he will have to decide how to gather. In addition, he will have to institute operational measures for measuring the independent, or A, value. In many cases this value can be viewed as a treatment or influence that is to be applied and measured. Again, there may be a difference of opinion concerning the measure's validity.

For both these measures, the difference of opinion about the validity, acceptability, and practicality are not matters that can be resolved by fiat. These issues go to the heart of the research design. More research is rejected in the end for alleged faulty measures than for any other single cause. If the researcher is not measuring what he claims he is measuring, there is no point to all his effort.

The tendency is often to leave this matter entirely in the hands of research specialists. It is the criminal justice professional, however, who must present his conclusions to the world. To properly sustain his position, the professional is well advised to become familiar with all the pros and cons of the ultimate choice for measurement. Otherwise he may be reduced to lamely saying "that he depended totally on the "experts"—or even more awkwardly that he had had doubts about the method, but said nothing. If, on the other hand, he has carefully followed the various rationales for the chosen, and the discarded, operational measures, he is in a much stronger position and can comfortably reveal that he has given mature consideration to an important issue. Ultimately, the choice of measures is a value judgment. Without a rationale for the interim choices, however, the way is open to irrebutable criticism.

Data Discipline

The intrusion of unnecessary and unwanted variables into the inquiry, as has been said, can only add to the problems caused by error. Setting up careful procedures to reduce the number of these unwanted variables is necessary if the influence of the A on the B is to be observed as a clear pattern without extraneous patterns obscuring existing relationships.

The interposition of personal bias in data collection is a prime source of error, and it should be minimized by mechanizing these procedures. Personal bias, random errors, consistent errors, and others can be reduced greatly by formalizing all schedules, eliminating personal judgments about the inclusion or exclusion of data, and so on. The administrator must be very inquisitive, for many researchers tend to take it for granted that there is no danger of personal bias if the data collectors are informed of the purpose of the research. Any criminal justice professional would be aware that probably the opposite is true.

Data is obtained from humans and by humans, analyzed by humans, and presented and used by humans. Bias, self-interest (fancied and real), fatigue, confusion, physiology, and perception are all at odds with accuracy when humans are concerned. Insofar as criminal justice is concerned, the barrenness of research that Norbert Wiener complains of[4] seems to be the product not of detective-mindedness of the lords of scientific administration, but rather by the lack of understanding and consideration for human frailty, and the lack of use of detective and auditing procedures.

Procedures

Because this book is devoted to general guidelines, research procedures will be outlined only briefly here. Specific techniques are described in great detail in books listed in the bibliography. From the criminal justice professional's point of view, however, he should *not* choose a research method because it appeals to him, then reach for a problem. He should start with the problem. Once his problem is fairly analyzed, he needs a guide to which method is likely to be the most useful.

In almost every case, the professional's first step should be to survey the accessible literature to determine the problem's place in the matrix of such problems, or at least to see how it has been discussed before. Only in this way can a science develop in criminal justice. The next consideration is the purpose, time, and resources that are available.

There is no real need under any ordinary circumstance to skip any part of the scientific approach, whatever method of data collection is ultimately settled on. Historical methods, library research, and all ex post facto methods always apply to some degree. The if-A-then-B model of hypothesis is invariably useful at this point and later. The same self-critical methods apply, and the problems of sampling and matching control groups are always excruciatingly present. Though the researcher has no control of past events, he can search among them for control situations to compare with influence situations that parallel his hypotheses.

A suitable calculation of probability of error in sampling and control groups can put that evidence into perspective. The dissimilarity of groups chosen in the past as compared with groups presently under concern is obvious, but their degree of dissimilarity can be estimated in the same ways that other groups can be compared. Admittedly, however, there may be less accuracy. Any research conducted should include the usual numerical estimations, calculated by qualified people. The mathematics are beyond this book, but appropriate texts are referenced in the bibliography.

The major concern in all research of this character, however, is to carefully differentiate between primary and secondary sources. Primary sources are the observations recorded at the time of their occurrence; secondary sources are all other records.

Another important point in historical approaches is to conduct two separate inquiries into both the verification of documents as well as the verification of the information contained in those documents.

Finally, it is recommended that all ex post facto research be supplemented by some empirical inquiry on the current scene, if only to verify the pertinence of the findings.

Contemporary descriptive approaches avoid the problems posed by the fog of time. The researcher can directly observe events, far more accurately match sample and control groups, personally query subjects, participate in the events he observes, and thus obtain subjective data with all the insight and error familiar to such data. Or he can observe events *indirectly* by their effects and their consequences. Subjects can be directed to perform, projective techniques can be used, interaction can be observed, and measures by the score can be devised for almost any independent or dependent variable. Generally, the term "descriptive" tends to mean noninterference in the subjects of research, as distinguished from the experimental method, in which strenuous efforts are made to control all variables except the particular independent and dependent variables under investigation.

Experimental situations involving human subjects, however, are difficult to create, and involve many serious questions of invasion of privacy. Many large institutions devoted to research have established standards for the protection of human subjects involved in investigations.[5] The standards are designed to protect knowing and unknowing participants in an experiment from exploitation. They restrict the research effort, but in a democratic society even the drive for knowledge must bend its methods to the larger benefits deriving from allegiance to the humanist tradition.[6]

Universe, Populations, and Samples

In-depth inquiry into a single case does not provide assurance that the findings can be generalized to other groups. Nevertheless, such "one-shot" occurrences may provide insight into deep-lying influences on critical situations, which can point the way to a more formal inquiry. But the inquiry into aggressive patrol, for example, would be unlikely to provide much information that could be generalized to other instances in other communities.

This generalization from a small group to a larger one necessitates a procedure called "sampling." Sampling involves the previously discussed research concepts of sets, universe, and population.

In sampling, population is defined as the entire group of values of a particular attribute of a universe of elements. The attribute of sex, which applied to every element in the universe of people, was expressed as the population of sex-values as they pertained to each element in the universe. Another previously discussed population was that of the attribute of friendship. This population of values was allocated to each element as friend or nonfriend.

There are, of course, many different attributes that the universe of people can be viewed as "possessing." As a set of values of one of these attributes is established, another population is noted. Each universe, then, "contains" many populations of attribute-values, along separate dimensions. A sample, in these terms can be defined as a subset of *one* of these populations. Clearly, the values of one population have no necessary relation to the values of any other population, even though they be of the same universe.

If, as has been said, each universe has many populations—each of a separate dimension—a sample of one of the populations has no necessary relevance to a sample of another population. For example, a sample of women from the population of sex-values of people would not reveal, in itself, whether any of the women are, or are not, friends. Each population is a separate entity—a separate set of attributes—or a separate dimension.

A very common error in sampling is to take a sample from one population of attributes and to try to apply findings from that sample to a different population of attributes than the one from which the sample was taken.

For instance, by unspecified means, a sample of 100 patrolmen is taken from the universe of 20,000 patrolmen in the New York Police Department. These patrolmen are weighed, and a sample of 100 weight-values is thus taken from the entire population of 20,000 weight-values. Will the arithmetic mean of the weight-values of the sample equal the arithmetic mean of the entire population of weight-values?

At this point it is not certain. One could, however, go out and weigh every patrolman in the NYPD and calculate the arithmetic mean from that data. It might be found that the sample provided a very close approximation, say, within 1 percent of the mean weight of the entire population of police-weights. But that finding has no relation at all to any other population; for example, it does not mean that the ratio of blonds and brunets of the police sample will be within 1 percent of the ratio of blonds and brunets of the universe of patrolmen.

Weight-values and hair-color-values are different dimensions. Whatever method was used that produced a sample so closely representative along the weight dimension may have an intrinsic bias in selection along the hair-color dimension. There is no way of knowing.

This is the type of sampling error that occurred in two presidential polls in the United States. The 1936 presidential election, between Franklin D. Roosevelt and Alfred M. Landon, was predicted to favor Landon by a landslide, but the result was opposite.

Analyzing the occurrence in if-A-then-B model form indicates that it may have been hypothesized that if a large enough sample of electors (A) were drawn, the vote they indicated would be reasonably close to the vote of all the electors (B).

Appropriate tests were made to satisfy the poll-takers that when electors indicated their preference on a survey taken the summer before an election, they consistently voted the same way in November. A sample size of 2 million was determined as being more than enough to obtain representative results.

The method was tried out in the presidential elections of 1920, 1924, 1928, and 1932, and it worked quite well. The 1936 sample, however, was drawn from automobile registration lists and telephone directories. That is, it was drawn along a dimension of the population of attributes that might be described as "having enough money to own a car or a telephone."

Unfortunately for those who drew up this research-design, the voters who went to the booths that autumn of economic depression were much more numerous along another dimension, which might be called "not having enough money to own either a car or a telephone."

The results were disastrous for the pollsters, and eventually *Literary Digest*, which had sponsored the poll, went out of business.

There were many potential errors and extraneous variables. The researchers saw them; they tried to assure corrections for such possible errors as the interviewees' refusal to indicate their true state of mind in a pre-election poll by various pretesting procedures. They brought the time of the inquiry as close as possible to the time of the election to minimize any changes in the political climate between survey date and actual election time. Great care was taken to reach for proper geographical representation so that voters in sparsely populated states were fairly represented, but not overrepresented in comparison with voters from more densely populated states.

The coincidence that the method had given correct results on four previous occasions was persuasive. The most expensive and learned people were available to do the most sophisticated analyses of the data. In the end, however, all precautions failed because they were operating in the wrong dimension. (The fiasco in forecasting the results of the 1948 Dewey-Truman election was the result of a similar flaw in sampling procedure.)

Sampling, then, can be said to be taking a portion of a population and assuming that it is representative. It involves two basic assumptions:

1. The population from which the sample is drawn is the same population to which conclusions, or results, will be generalized.
2. The sample is representative of the population from which it is drawn.

Sometimes the fact that the sample is not from the population in which we are really interested is not apparent as in the presidential polling cases.

Another error is frequently encountered in sampling: Even though the sample is drawn from the same population as the one to which the researcher will generalize, it may not have the same proportional pattern of those attributes as the population. However earnest the effort, however judicious the decisions to include elements from each of the known groups in the universe or population, there is no way to calculate the degree of representativeness unless the entire population is listed and measured.

There is tremendous pressure in the real world of criminal justice to take "samples of convenience." Such practice is all right as long as it is consciously the result of tradeoffs of costs and benefits. Clearly acknowledging such decisions and the degree of arbitrariness involved will tend to mitigate the evil effects of overgeneralization from sample results. From the scientific view, however, the objection to such "judgment" samples is that there is no way to anticipate the degree of error.

There is another way of selecting samples, however, and although it does not guarantee a more representative subset, it does permit the calculation of the probability that any deviations from representativeness are merely random error, and not a "real" difference.

This sample-selection process is called "random sampling." It is a necessary preliminary to the application of mathematical methods that will give estimates called "standard error" that can be used as the measure against which the outcomes of investigations can be checked. That is, it is possible to fix limits above and below a sample value, and to assert with a known degree of confidence that the population value falls within those limits, which are known as "confidence limits."

For example, assume a jar is filled with 100 pennies. If a person reaches blindly into the jar, withdraws two pennies, and slams them down on a table under his hand without looking at them, what is the chance that there are two heads? Considering that there are four possible ways the pennies could appear—head-tail, head-head, tail-head, and tail-tail—there is one chance out of four.

If the coins appear as head-head, the sample is *not* representative of the ratio of heads to tails of the entire population in the jar. If the sample is head-tail or tail-head, however, it would be exactly representative, as defined. Furthermore, that sample combination would be expected to occur only 50 percent of the time. That is, half of the time it would be exactly representative, and the other half of the time it would deviate in one direction or another.

Thus while the sample is not guaranteed to be representative, with a considerable degree of confidence it can be expected to be correct 50 percent of the time. At least *some* certainty has come out of uncertainty.

Of course this does not mean that if four samples are taken, two of them would be exactly representative. It merely means that theoretically, in the long run one would expect 50 percent of the samples to be truly representative. When these theoretical calculations are checked in practice, they appear with great regularity. In practical sampling, while random variability of each element is unpredictable by definition, the variability of a random sample *is* predictable.

Since in most occasions in real life the actual characteristics of the population are never known—because they are so numerous as to be too costly to be measured—a researcher must depend on his knowledge of samples. He must assume that what can be inferred or observed about samples is "probably" the fact about populations.

There is nothing startling about this: A citizen may "know" police are "good" because policemen of the sample with whom he is acquainted are "good." Other citizens may "know" police are "bad" because they have so inferred from the sample with which they are acquainted.

It is a great advance in knowledge, however, when it is possible to state with precision the probability in numerical terms that a sample will give a correct impression, within a specific confidence limit. It is perhaps not much more than before—but at least it is possible to know how reliable original impressions are.

How, then, is this scientifically desirable state of randomness attained? What *orders* do we issue, to attain a state completely without order?

Within the framework of probability theory, "random" refers to a situation where each element has an equal chance of being selected. This "equiprobability" is basic in scientific sampling theory and manipulations of the statistics based on it.

The theoretical condition of random arrangement can be operationalized satisfactorily by a number of methods (all start with listing each element):

1. Listing each element of the population on a card; thoroughly shuffling the cards; dealing off the size sample desired
2. Listing the digits from 0, 1, 2, and so on, to 9, on slips of paper; thoroughly mixing them; drawing one slip at a time; marking the digit drawn on a matrix with as many columns as are needed to enumerate each element in the population; applying these random numbers to the list of all elements in the population; selecting the sample size needed by taking elements no. 1 through the number that represents the sample size needed (the reverse of this procedure would also be acceptable: listing the elements on the matrix, and selecting the sample by choosing among them from a random-number list)
3. Using a random number table from a book of such tables (a variation of method 2)
4. Programming an electronic computer to produce a flow of random numbers that can be used as in method 2.

Standing on a corner and "randomly" selecting passers-by is not random in the sense required for a scientific sample. Nor is it satisfactory to "randomly" pick names from a list. The sources of error are obvious.

When statisticians say that "the sample does not differ from the population significantly," they do not mean that the sample is representative. They mean only that the sample probably does not differ from the population, to a degree that can be considered "important."

The entire randomness process is an attempt to make predictable in the aggregate a series of events that are completely unpredictable individually. To reiterate: If each element of the population has an equal chance of being selected for the sample, it is a random sample.

Summarizing the entire random sampling process:

1. A precise definition of the population must be made.

2. A complete list of the defined population must be obtained.
3. A selection procedure must be set up that equalizes each element's chance to be selected for the sample.

Despite the theoretical value of random sampling, the criminal justice professional will repeatedly be exposed to researches that use various types of "judgment" samples.

For example, use will often be made of a sample of residents of, say, Dade County, Florida, selected with the following rationale: Since the total population of Dade is about 1,500,000, and about 350,000 of these are of Cuban descent, a sample will be drawn in which Cubans are chosen to be in the proportion to the total population of 350,000/1,500,000, or about 70 out of a sample size of 300. Selections of other ethnic or national-origin groups will be similarly proportionately represented.

The utility of the sample for criminal justice purposes, however, assumes that ethnicity is a relevant attribute in the if-A-then-B model of presumed influence. If that assumption is valid, quite useful results may occur, but there is no way to calculate the likelihood of success. Nevertheless, convenience will often rule, which is all right as long as one knows the risks, accepts them, and does not pretend to an unjustified "scientific" representativeness by attempting to use confidence limits or other statistical calculation founded on randomness in the sample.

A general approach to evaluating the sampling methods cited in research reports would be to estimate the cost of a true random sample as an upper limit for both costs and desirability. The next step would be to estimate the most likely stratification that will avoid major errors, by providing representation for a fair balance of the relevant attributes. Finally, a rigorous randomness among those strata can conclude the procedure.

For example, now that we know that occupation and income are relevant to voting patterns, pollsters make sure there is a proportionate representation of each occupation and income level in their samples. Then they randomize among these strata to locate particular sample elements. Thus far, such randomized stratification seems to have produced reasonably acceptable results.

The various ratings granted television programs are the result of another system, which is rather carefully concealed. The fact of concealment, itself, is sufficient to make it suspect. Suspect because any inquiry which does not reveal its methods and data so as to permit complete replication can make no claim to being scientific.

Sample Size

How large should a sample be? The theory of probability predicts that if other things are equal, representativeness will be a function of the relative sizes of the sample and the population.

If the population is not large, a sample of 10 percent of the population may be hardly sufficient. Even then, significant elements or attributes may not be represented. Nevertheless, the theory is, as long as there was an equal chance of representation, the requirements of random sample design are met.[7] On the other hand, if the population is large, a much smaller percentage than 10 percent may give accurate results with a low probability of error.

There are tables that summarize the relationships between various sizes of population and sample, with the confidence limits in such cases. There are also rules of thumb to determine minimum recommended sample sizes. One good guide is to remember that the cells in a crossbreak should average at least ten values. It would be better if the cells average twenty or more, to lessen the probability that a low count would be given more consideration than it deserves. As one might say, "To give randomization a chance to work."

This does not mean that a crossbreak should not exhibit empty cells, but merely that the sample size should be twenty or more times the number of cells in the crossbreak that is being used. If the sample size is insufficient, it is advisable to reduce the size of the crossbreak. In contrast, a crossbreak with many cells will require a large sample to produce credible results. Of course, other factors may affect the decision about sample size. There may just be not enough equivalent elements available, costs may limit sample size, and time or other facilities may be in short supply.

To calculate the number of cells that will be in a proposed crossbreak, multiply the number of values in each dimension—e.g., a 3 X 3 X 3 crossbreak will display twenty-seven cells, and a 2 X 3 crossbreak will cross-tabulate to six cells.

Generally, the larger the sample the greater the resemblance to the population, if it is a finite number. Too often, however, populations are such large numbers that one cannot rely on merely large samples to attain accuracy, or even to reduce bias. Very large samples may calculate to a statistically significant result even though the if-A-then-B relationship may be too slight to be important to a practitioner.

Whether a given research into a criminal justice problem should take the route of a stratified random, a judgment, or merely a convenient sample—or even to reach for a truly random sample is a sticky question. The parameters of this decision are given here. Advice should be sought from experts in statistics and in the specific problem area. The ultimate decision will affect the research unalterably.

Usually pragmatism will rule. Nevertheless, obviously erroneous methods should be avoided whenever possible, or given due weight when unavoidable. It is wise to try for randomness even when a truly "equal probability of selection" cannot be attained. The effort encourages rigor and skepticism and a salutary effort to eschew "judgment" about the inclusion of elements, or populations. Choice should be randomized as much as possible. The "convenient" sample is simply the hope that ignorance is bliss; it becomes the rule only when a lazy researcher leads the way.

It is important to remember, however, that randomness does not ensure representativeness. It can provide only an estimate of the size of the probable error.[8]

Probability thinking is applied in every procedure in science, especially in sampling. It enters at every level—experimental samples, control samples, assignments of treatments, or types of treatments (it can even help decide whether there is to be any treatment at all).

Randomness, and its presumed or actual consequences, are used constantly in measurements, in evaluation, and in decision-making of every kind. Its use in research design is only one facet of this phenomenon. The criminal justice practitioner must make probability, and the language of probability, his familiar tool. He will use it not only to estimate the likelihood of a decision's being correct or incorrect, but also to evaluate how serious the consequences of accepting an incorrect decision, or rejecting a correct decision.

These matters will be treated in detail in Chapter 6, particularly in regard to hypothesis testing, but a short preview example would be to consider that even though a person charged with crime under certain conditions can be shown to exhibit the same characteristics that would indicate an 80-percent probability of guilt (in that 80 times out of 100 such cases guilt has been proven previously), the jury's decision must be to dismiss the charges because the cost to the defendant is too great. In a murder charge, the cost would be the maximum penalty, perhaps execution.

A decision may be too costly, should it be wrong—even though the chance of its being correct may be as high as 95 percent or even 99 percent—if it would mean the loss of the decision-maker's own job, or great danger to the public.[9] An example of the latter might be a small pilot program involving disarming the police, showing a "significantly high" probability of improved public relations and "significantly low" probability of injury to police or public. Let us suppose these findings are reached after an appropriately rigorous, controlled experiment. Even though the findings may be valid in every way, the cautious professional decision-maker in criminal justice would not be advised to recommend that the entire police department undertake to cast away their arms. However remote the chance of disaster, the careful decision would be to proceed very, very slowly—if at all.

This balancing of research findings and probabilities, with practical considerations of costs and consequences, is the heart of criminal justice decision-making.[10]

4 Data Collection

Can we be sure of what we mean? One way is a ruthless purge of sentiment. We can do that by thinking only in terms of operations.

Bridgman
The Nature of Some of Our Physical Concepts
The Way Things Are

The statement from Bridgman is perhaps best understood if paraphrased to read "Can *others* be sure of what we mean?" The only way others can be sure of what we mean is by what we do. In research, this is called "operationalizing."[1]

Thus one may say "intelligence," but if what one does is to offer a score from an intelligence test, what is really meant is not intelligence, but that score on that particular instrument.

Basic Problems

Process Becomes Goal

A criminal justice professional may say he manages an "efficient" police department, but if what he offers as "proof" is that a certain number of arrests per man-hour of patrol was effected in the current year, that bit of data is what he means.[2] He has transformed whatever may have been in his mind, in use of "operations" (in Bridgman's term), to an organizational goal of simply attaining more arrests per man-hour of patrol.

The original objective was to have an efficient police department. It now has become an objective in translation to operations, and the operation has become the objective: process has become goal. Every member of that department now *knows* that efficiency will be measured by the criterion of arrests per patrol-hours. Unfortunately, from the knowledge that the entire department's efficiency is measured by that ratio, there is an inevitable shift to accepting the conclusion that each unit in that department, or even every patrol officer's efficiency, will be measured by that ratio. This fault is grievous, but common.

The same applies to the collection of data. The research design designates the goal of data collection and then presents an operationalized statement of exactly what is to be done to attain that goal by gathering data in certain ways and places.

At the beginning, it is easy when designing the research plan, to keep in mind what is obvious: that the particular data-collection process designated as the operationalized research goal is perhaps only one out of dozens of possible procedures that might have been used. Each one of those procedures—all unchosen—probably would have produced different findings than the one selected. Nevertheless, the chosen method becomes the ultimate measure and tends to take on a goal-like quality. It becomes the object of the entire research effort, and thereafter it often will become unquestioned in validity and infallible in decision.

This, of course, is accepting the shadow for the substance. Robert K. Merton's numerous comments about goal displacement in organizations place this problem in a context familiar to criminal justice professionals.[3] Even without being familiar with the extensive literature on goal displacement, every administrator has experienced the reality of it within his own organization. The insidious phenomenon is no different in data collection, and it is to be guarded against in much the same way as in all criminal justice organizations.

The first rule is to openly and clearly admit to the arbitrariness of the particular operationalized measure. The admission must first come by those in the research before it comes from any outside the group assigned to the inquiry. Too often research people become obsessed with the seeming *truth* of their measures. Their intellects shut off, and their ideologies rule.

One can sympathize with the enthusiasm with which unexpected happy discoveries become persuasive to onlookers and participants. For really useful research, however, skepticism is a more reliable attitude.

Audit

Practically all the problems of data collection reduce to (1) following the dictates of the research design rigidly, and (2) constantly auditing to affirm it.

If this book has one firm conviction to convey, it is that data-collection policies and procedures should be audited constantly—in the field, in the office, in the computer room, and then all over again.

One cannot give too much care to ascertain that the discipline for collection procedures laid down by the research design is actually carried out, for error can creep in at every turn.

Twenty-five centuries ago the art of administration had reached a far higher stage of development than the art of medicine. By then, magnificent accomplishments in organization of human effort for common goals had reached high levels in the works at Karnak, the Great Wall of China, and in the field operations of such noted historical figures as Cyrus, Alexander, the Roman generals and their opponent Hannibal, continuing through the period of Genghis Khan and other military and government figures. In many respects, the modern science of government and human organization is no more advanced than it was thousands of years ago.

On the other hand, medicine, from the inception of Hippocrates' scientific observational techniques, has shown continuous advance, firmly founded processes that permit theories to be born and undergo numerous mutations. Case studies and records of observations collected by Hippocrates are still cited today in medical works.

Accurate, permanently recorded observations are the foundation stones of a growing science, but government has been built on quicksand. Without objective, impartial factual data, we read of Richelieu, Lyautey, Walpole, Fouché, and Bismark as skilled practitioners, but we are unable fully to comprehend their deeds. There are many political statements from their time, but little that can be set forth as objective facts pointing the way to a theory of administration. Nor were there any solid theoretical statements from them.

Without having recourse to comparative factual data, the theories of Machiavelli remain unchallenged at the research level by those of Mao Tse-tung, Woodrow Wilson, Douglas MacGregor, or Saul Alinsky.

Without firm facts to anchor it, theory, like ideology, is free to fly to whatever metaphysical world it may. The gift of science has been the uniting of theory to fact, checking the erratic flight of imagination with the steadying influence of empirical observation and measurement.

When criminal justice has amassed a solid mass of empirical, controlled observation, it will have a rock embedded in reality. On this it will be possible to erect a true science of criminal justice.

There are few if any "facts" in criminal justice that are not corrupted by bias. Operationalization of behavioral measurement appears to run risks that are not run in the physical sciences. The focus of concern in criminal justice is humanity—a changeable, malleable, vital, stubborn thing, perhaps beyond the understanding of mortals.

Some of the ways that facts about people have been collected have been listed under phrases that are self-descriptive in their simplicity, but there are numerous details in their execution, which are best left to reference texts:[4] participant-observation; interviewing; questionnaire surveys; case studies; role analysis; sociometry; descriptive studies; historical research; experimental research; and semantic differential analysis, to name only several. There are also theoretical orientations such as Lewin's field theory, and group dynamics. The list is almost endless, because new types are invented daily—such as content analysis, interaction process, and projective techniques—all in new guises and variations.

The research design will prescribe whether these or other patterns will be the route the data collection will take.

Each one of these methods has, on occasion, been used when it has been contraindicated, because the method's basic assumptions or technique were violated by the nature of the hypotheses involved. Thorough review must be made, via impartial advice from experts in the proposed method, of rationale, weaknesses, and strengths as compared to other methods. It would be wise to review a reference text at the same time. There is no general strong method.

Too often, immature research has been instituted on the basis of a previously chosen, preferred method, rather than on a fair examination of all available methods. Thus surveys and opinionnaires tend to be overworked by undergraduate research students, even when less familiar techniques would have been more applicable.

Relevant questions that have to be answered at the same time as review of available instruments and methodology for data collection are: In what form will the data be? Will there be items to be counted? Will there be imponderables such as attitudes or opinions to be estimated? What can be measured? Is it relevant to the hypotheses? What degree of accuracy is needed?

A first rule should be to beware of one researcher, one method, *or* one instrument. The point is not to prove that the hypothesis is *correct*, but to *find out* something. To rely on a single approach is to be shackled. A survey, for instance, can *never* really draw a sample of a previously defined universe. Inevitably, the survey-sample is composed of only those people who were willing to respond. Nonrespondents may be quite different from the respondents, which is why such surveys as the Kinsey Report received such violent opposition. This report was never replicated, on doubtful logical ground in the first instance, what could have been a valuable resource, to students of sociology and society has given the field over to 'activists' of one kind or another.

On the other hand, the researcher should avoid intricate theories and taxonomies. However good they may look on paper, they are merely window-dressing unless they solve the problem. This does not mock the acknowledged complexity of reality—it is merely that intricate theories defy setting forth testable hypotheses. Order and simplification are the steps toward mastering the unknown. It is theoretically possible to analyze for the influence of 10, 20, or even 50 or 100 different variables, but the effort will be fruitless for our finite understanding. To trace through the vagaries of more than about 4 variables just does not work out at the present stage of even computerized analytical ability.

The researcher should never exclude any data whatsoever, once the search is started. However ridiculous the item may appear, it should be included in the data unless there is very good reason not to do so. In any case the circumstances should be noted in detail. What appears to be merely an accidental incident with no relation to the hypothesis at an early stage may be an open door to an important discovery.

Finally, all original data, all documentation of whatever kind, all statements of rationale, all decisions, and all errors must be carefully catalogued, stored, and made available to all reasonable research inquiries.

What Can Be Measured?

The only thing worth measuring, and the only thing that can be measured, is *difference*. Measuring is not done in an absolute sense, but by comparing one thing with another to note the difference between the two.

But a researcher must guard against measuring differences that are merely the result of error. Consequently, considering what can be measured is never far from anticipating the potential errors in the measurement. How can errors be balanced out, found, and controlled?

Because measurement involves comparisons, the researcher must start with a search for base comparison groups. If the comparison groups come from the universe of his concern, he has the beginning of internal validity. If the comparison groups come from outside the universe, however, he is reaching for validation beyond his ken, toward further generalization, a more encompassing statement of the value of his efforts.

Comparison groups are usually chosen by a judgmental process. Certainly, this process loses the benefits of randomization in terms of calculating the probability of error. Generally, the randomization of control groups will call for large numbers of such groups to choose from, and large numbers of elements in each group—to the extent that randomization becomes too costly. Whatever the decision, it should be carefully noted in the research design, with clear written statements giving the reasons for the choice.

Costs are significantly higher when dealing with large groups, and under the following circumstances, a judgment choice of comparison groups might be worthwhile:

1. If the entire universe of such groups can be viewed at the same time;
2. If the person doing the judging has demonstrated the ability to judge accurately in prior instances;
3. If the number of possible choices is relatively small, say, ten or so;
4. If each group is not too different from other groups along the relevant dimension.

However advisable for practical reasons a judgment is made, instead of randomization, research experience indicates this decision is weak statistically because (1) it is impossible to determine the probability that an element or a group will be selected, and (2) it is impossible to determine the degree of error in the data.

With a view to long-term benefits that might accrue from scientific approaches, it is generally better to accept more possible error, rather than insisting on, or guessing, the least possible error in a given instance *if* it is possible to calculate how much error is probable.

Thus it is recommended to use randomization for grouping or sampling, whenever practicable, especially if probable error will be computed. The benefits of randomization are so great that it should be used at least partially in almost every research effort. It tends to prevent the build-up of bias upon bias, and thus it reaches for impartiality. A possible negative consequence is that it may delude the research staff into thinking they have accomplished utter rigor.

Control Groups

One of the major reasons for using the if-*A*-then-*B* model is that it facilitates the comparison of differences between before and after "treatment." Since conceivably the phenomenon could occur due to a mere maturation or change process inherent in the subject over the period of the treatment, it would appear essential to maintain a group similar in constitution to the "treated" group that is completely exempt from the influence of *A*, the independent variable.

One cannot be completely certain that the control group that is *not* to receive treatment with *A* is really similar in constitution and nature to the treated, or experimental, group. But the problem can be approached in a scientific way by randomizing among *all* the members of that universe.

Granted, this method is less than perfect. Experience, however, has uncovered no better way. It may allay distrust of "matching" elements of the universe, or of matching element-attributes in the relevant population, to try to make the two groups equivalent. Unfortunately, it is quite likely that the very act or process of matching will introduce systematic bias. There is no guarantee that matching on one dimension will result in equal matching along another dimension.

However the groups for the research are selected, the simple "post-test only" design does not use control groups to their fullest to control error. It is possible to consider testing the group beforehand to determine if there is any determinable level of the phenomenon *B*. But then there would be the possibility that the act of testing has in some manner changed the group.

To avoid some of these problems, the most common experimental arrangement of control and experimental groups for research is the Solomon four-group design. In this arrangement of groups, randomization is used to select four "probably equivalent" groups. Two are randomly chosen to be experimental groups, that is, to be given the benefit of treatment with the independent variable. The other two are to be control groups.

One experimental group is given a pretest to determine the amount of preexisting *B* attributes. The same is done to one of the control groups. Again, these choices should be made randomly.

The *A* treatment is then applied to the previously selected experimental groups. Immediately thereafter, a post-test is made of all four groups for the presence or absence of the *B* variable.

The pattern can be diagrammed as shown in Figure 4-1. In the figure, groups 1 and 3 are experimental groups because they are the ones that received application of the *A* variable, or treatment. Groups 2 and 4 are control groups because they did not receive treatment with the *A* variable. Any changes over time noted in groups 2 and 4 could be due to variables *other* than the influence of *A*.

If change is noted in the control groups that did not receive *A* treatment—say, a learning experience—one must infer that the change must be due to some other influence. Possibly it is the result of learning outside of the experimental situation, or an internal developmental change in the subjects, or another unknown factor. An example would be the improvement in levels of knowledge and skill that a child exhibits at the beginning of a school year over his level the year before, whether or not he attended school regularly. Presumably the child learns even without the *A* variable treatment of formal schooling. Of course he may learn different things, but often the post-test will show a considerable advance in learning on almost any *B* variables used in the post-test.

The Solomon four-group pattern of pretest-treatment-post-test is deemed the most satisfactory of simple research group arrangements. However, there are many other patterns in use. Some of these patterns use six, eight, or many more groups, especially if it is known or suspected that differing amounts of treatment may give significantly different results on a post-test, in a nonlinear effect.

The comparatively simple Solomon four-group design permits gauging the effects of unknown variables and alternative hypotheses in many practical instances. However, the necessity for careful selection of the groups significantly increases the cost and difficulties over the one-group, "one-shot" inquiry—each of the four groups must meet the strictures of sample size, which call for, among other things, an optimum of twenty values for each cell in a crossbreak. It may be difficult to locate sufficient subjects of the same kind.

Time

Group	B	A	B
1	Pretest	Treatment	Post-test
2	Pretest		Post-test
3		Treatment	Post-test
4			Post-test

Figure 4-1. The Pretest–Treatment–Post-test Pattern.

The Solomon four-group design, however, does not solve all problems of control, even if sufficient subjects are available. This is one difficulty that is the subject of current inquiry.

While generally it seems reasonable that the more *treatment*, the more *effect*, there is the distinct possibility that the treatment will modify the effect in a nonlinear, noncumulative way.

For example, the more punches (A) the challenger delivers to the midsection of the champion in a given round, the more likely the champion will be knocked out (B). But that effect is not necessarily linear. Twice as many punches do not bring the challenger twice as close to winning by a knockout; nor is it necessarily true that the effect is cumulative at all. Often the fighter who receives the most punches and is close to being knocked out will suddenly revive and possibly even flatten the other fighter. Using symbols, A then B until A reaches a certain intensity, then B reverses.

There are complex multiple-group designs, and mathematical techniques that have only recently been developed to try to handle that kind of situation. These specialized discussions on catastrophe theory and other advanced concepts are too lengthy to be discussed here.[5]

Scaling and Measuring

Counting, a "digital" measure, conceives of each element as being of one kind, at least along the dimension or attributes of the A's or B's. Most people have no objection whatever to counting elements as a measure of quantity. It appears to be perfectly consonant with observation, prior experience, tradition, and intuition. However, there are a great number of characteristics of humans and objects for which there is no common agreement about either their intrinsic natures or the appropriate measures of them. Many doubt that some of these can ever be measured at all—for example, intelligence, achievement, attitude, honesty, anxiety, friendliness, cynicism, orderliness, ability, and potential of almost any kind. Other examples are human sensations, such as pain, taste, heat, stress, well-being, and fatigue.

Much of criminal justice is concerned with material matters that may be rather easily measured by counting objects or elements, or attributes that are easily reduced to elements, such as weight, distance, hardness, and rates or ratios of countable elements. There are occasions, however, when it would be useful to measure human characteristics, if it were only possible.

The behavioral sciences have grappled with this problem, and in so doing have developed many vocabularies and concepts. The comprehension of measurement problems depends on some familiarity with the language and principles of psychometrics.

A very broad definition of measurement is: The assignment of symbols to elements according to rules which permit comparisons.

Nominal Measurement

Comparing symbols of things to indicate "no relation" is called categorization, or nominal measurement. Thus each symbol is given a different name to distinguish it from the others.

One of the elements of the universe-set of, say, humans would be "human," just as "dog" would indicate one element of the universe of dogs. H could stand for the entire universe of humans, and H_1 would be one particular element in that universe. Such a convention would imply that H_2 would be another element in that same universe, and H_n would indicate *any* given element in that universe.

Using the same symbolic system, D would be the shorthand for the universe of dogs, and $D_1, D_2, D_3, \ldots, D_n$ would indicate a sequence of dog elements. It is clear that the names "humans" and "dogs," or H and D, indicate that there is a difference between them. Naming things distinguishes one thing from the other; the name categorically declares that there is no relation along the dimension of concern.

On closer examination, of course, a relationship may be found on another dimension. For example, the universe of people is nominally differentiated from the universe of friends. In a previous example, friends was a subset of the universe of people. Stating the name "people" and applying it to a universe, and likewise naming another universe "friends" does not, by such naming, reveal that one is the subset of the other. The names merely identify separate identities. They are separate, and they cannot be added or subtracted by the rules of arithmetic—you can't add apples and oranges. The *quality* of being a friend cannot be added to the *quality* of being a person.

Counting Measurement

Counting, as it is commonly known, fits the definition of measurement that has been given. After a researcher has named a universe, he can assign to each element a series of symbols to indicate whatever relationship he cares to communicate.

Numbers have a sequential relationship, such that the numbers from, say, 1 through 10 will follow in the specific order 1,2,3, and so on. The number 10 will correspond to the tenth element in the series. This rule of assignment, taken from the empirical world common to everyone, enables it to be said that the set of elements has a certain "count," in this case, ten, and that there are a total of *ten* elements in the set that has been named with those numbers.

In crossbreaks, an element can have a number of names, each along a different dimension, at the same time. Each name indicates an element's membership in a different universe. Thus an element in the previously mentioned crossbreak was simultaneously a member of the universes, or subsets, people, friends, and blonds. The terminology would be that the universe, U_1 of people could be counted, and that the populations friendship (P_1), sex (P_2), and hair color (P_3) could be counted, too.

Thus it is possible to count the elements of universes and attributes of populations, and the individual items of attributes can be considered as elements at their level—worlds within worlds.

Ordinal Measurement

If the assignment of numbers, as in the previous section, was temporary, all that is known is the total count. If, however, those numbers are assigned permanently, it has been designated which element is to come first in a rank-order, which second, and so on, to the tenth element in the order.

If the permanent assignment of rank-order indicates an empirical relationship, it is "ordinal measurement." Thus if a researcher wanted to indicate that there were different values of weights of patrolmen, he could assign subscript numbers in sequence to indicate this rank-order: for example, element W_1 being heavier than all the others, W_2 next heaviest, W_3 next, and so on to W_n.

The sequence could be reversed so that the first in the sequence would be lighter in weight than all the others, the second next lightest, and so on, as long as the intended meaning is indicated by the numbered rank-ordered sequence.

There is absolutely no imputation that number 5 in the series is five times as heavy as number 1 in the series, nor that it is half as heavy as 10. There is also no reason to believe that 2 is one pound, one kilogram, or one ton more than 1. Rank-order is independent of any unit of measurement at all, except that each rank denotes at least one element. Several elements, however, may be of the same rank, and therefore each element should be listed with its rank.

Patrolmen could be ranked by height, lung capacity, strength, and perhaps intelligence, all without recourse to any specific measurement unit. Comparison can be along other dimensions than human characteristics, such as "higher than," "arrived in station-house first," "number of arrests made by," or any other attribute. The only desideratum would be that there could be a comparison between a pair of patrolmen to determine which had more of the quality than the other.

Again, it is to be noted that rank-order does not permit conclusions about the distance between the intervals, nor about any relationship except rank. Ordinal measurement gives information about rank-order and nothing else.

Equal-Interval Measurement

Number symbols that represent equal intervals of an attribute's values can convey more information than mere ordinal measurement.[6] Thus in the empirical world of a police station-house, the back room may be filled with patrolmen whose heights can be discerned as measurable by one-inch intervals. If the shortest man is taken as a base, the next taller man would be noted as being one inch taller, the next man another inch taller still, until the tallest man is, say, ten inches taller than the shortest.

Now the men are ranked in order, and in addition the scores can be added or subtracted to find the interval distance. Interestingly, the score of any man, subtracted from the score of any other man, will give the interval distance in a score that will be equivalent to the difference in height.

In fact, all operations of addition and subtraction can be performed on the scores of such equal-interval scales. (But the scores are not the actual heights of the patrolmen.) Equal-interval scores cannot be multiplied or divided, however. For example, a patrolman who is ten inches taller than the shortest patrolman is certainly not ten times taller, nor is his score ten times the base score.

Ratio Measurement

The equal-interval scale gave useful information, but it could not give a fair comparison on a ratio level. That is, there was no way to discover the absolute relationship between the height of the shortest patrolman and the height of the tallest patrolman. This was because there was no absolute or *natural* zero, where there was no actual height at all.

Taking the height of the shortest patrolman as a base gave an artificial baseline, or artificial zero, which did not interfere with estimating score intervals or with adding or subtracting inches of height. But the artificial zero had negated any possibility of estimating the ratio of one height with another.

That problem is resolved by putting the zero where it belongs. This can be done by making a scale starting with zero height and increasing in value by one-inch intervals, up to, say, 78 inches. If scores of the patrolmen's heights are placed on this scale, they can be divided or multiplied: ratio estimations can be made. The mathematical language now represents the natural world. A patrolman who is 78 inches tall is also 10/68 taller than a patrolman who is 68 inches tall. A patrolman who is 73 inches tall is 5/68 taller than the 68-inch-tall policeman, and a 78-inch-tall patrolman is 5/73 taller than the 73-inch-tall patrolman, and so on.

Unless there is a natural zero, the ratios between the scores may not be taken to mean any specific thing about reality. A ratio scale can be subjected to all arithmetic operations, including multiplication and division, as well as addition and subtraction.

These very obvious attributes of ratio-scales are important because while it is simple to find a natural zero for attributes such as height, weight, distance, or volume, many of the attributes dealt with in psychometrics show no absolute or natural zero. Who has zero personality? What does "zero intelligence" mean? These attributes are hypothetical constructs, with no clear definition other than arbitrary imagination devises and "operationalizes" in the form of a scale and a test.

Thus often in measuring human characteristics, a researcher may opt to base the definition of the characteristic on the scale he has devised to measure it. But the scale is invented, in the first instance, on a conceptual definition of the characteristic as he envisages it. Thus he has reached complete circularity.

For example, a researcher may say that he is not measuring intelligence, he is measuring whatever the test instrument measures, which is all right because the results correlate very well with success in college, which is the thing in which he is interested.[7]

In this circumstance there is no natural or absolute zero on the scale used in such a test instrument. There is therefore no ratio scale. There usually is even doubt that it is an equal-interval scale—though often it will be assumed, for purposes of justifying the use of certain analytical techniques, that an equal-interval scale does exist.

Assuming the existence of equal-interval scales seems to have provided much information that has been "useful" to researchers. Certainly that is no reason for criminal justice professionals to be unaware of the leap into speculation that is involved. The best advice is to look into it in every case, and to insist on clear documentation of every element of assumption and potential extraneous variance.

Even though on occasion a psychometric scale may be treated as an equal-interval scale, on no account should such a scale be used to compare operations involving multiplication or division because they are not natural-zero scales.

These matters unfortunately have not been obvious to some researchers. Frequently, papers that purport to present data fairly have ignored the fact that there are no ratio scales in psychometrics.

Most psychometric scales are ordinal, in the opinion of the most careful researchers. It does appear reasonable to compare intelligence quotients, as scores, to discover which is higher. By successive pair-comparisons an ordinal scale of scores can be constructed.

There is room for considerable discretion as to how far a researcher should go in treating an ordinal scale as an equal-interval scale. There are technical statistical means for trying to solve this problem, but there is no certainty in such decisions either.

Criminal justice professionals are forced to inquire of qualified statisticians' opinions regarding their evaluation of the seriousness of the errors involved in using specific scales beyond their intrinsic data content. All findings in reports should reveal this value judgment. Any outreach to speculative conclusions should repeat the warnings about the possibility of scaling distortion.

All these scales, when applied in research to measure any attribute of varying value, must be carefully reviewed in their particular situation, in the light of the concepts in Thurstone's law of comparative judgment, and skeptical good sense.[8]

It may be expeditious to hazard variance to get *some* results, even though they may be erroneous—but one should not be unconscious of the possibility of error.

Types of Rating Scales[9]

The basic problem in developing rating scales is to divide an attribute-dimension into a quantitative series, or as researchers say, to order items along a continuum.

Frequently it is easy to obtain common agreement about the identity of a dimension of social or human characteristics, even about what are observed to be *differences* in individuals along that dimension. It becomes more difficult to assign a quantitative value to one observation in relation to another observation. Such paired comparisons, however, are much more easily come by than the ordering of a series of five or more ranked values of different dimensions.

For example, in trying to discover a local community's attitude toward a police department, suppose that all of the following are accepted as relevant dimensions: (1) number of civilian complaints against police in a given period, (2) number of favorable letters praising police action, and (3) scores on an opinionnaire given to a representative sample of the community.

Each of these dimensions is different, yet presumably each is a reasonable measure of community attitude. How does one equate, say, a certain high number of civilian complaints with a large number of letters praising police action? How do both those measures add up with the scores on the opinionnaire?

The opinionnaire itself, if it is like many of them, will have a number of questions calling for responses to queries such as: (1) The last you saw a policeman, was he doing something you thought was properly his job? (2) Are policemen paid too much for what they do? (3) Do policemen customarily talk or act discourteously? (4) Do policemen do their best to suppress crime?

What does it mean if the respondent answers yes to all four questions on the opinionnaire? Presumably, "yes" in response to questions 2 and 3 indicates a negative feeling about police, and "yes" in response to questions 1 and 4 reveals a positive attitude. Does the even split in answers indicate a passive attitude? In other words, are each of the four questions worthy of equal weight?

Actually, the dimensions explored by each question can be viewed as being quite different from each other. Nevertheless, are they close enough to permit the extraction of information that would aid a police administrator in evaluating his department's image? In other words, is there a dimension such as the one being sought? Or are there a number of dimensions, so closely related, that they can be included in the scale without destroying continuity?

Problems such as these have been encountered in the study of attitudes, potential for performance, operational practices, and many other areas. A great many techniques have been developed to deal with them, and new methods are devised almost daily.

A criminal justice professional can use his experience to prevent a relative newcomer to the justice scene from gross error, by helping him determine just what it is that will be measured—what A's and what B's. Justification for the dimension adopted must be presented in logical form for criticism by all concerned, knowledgeable persons—not only for the general thesis of the research, but also for each scaled item used to approach the major thesis. In short, one must "prove" the major dimension, the scaled dimensions, and the values of the continua used.

Scales, measures, and tests are merely three ways of saying measuring instruments. There are, however, some connotative implications of each word: "test" implies success or failure, or at least competition, "measure" implies a quantitative reality; and "scale" is also used to refer to the set of numbers on any measuring instrument.

An "objective" test or scale is one in which there is a very high degree of probability (+99.9 percent) that all persons following the prescribed rules will assign the same scaled values to the items, *and* that all persons scoring the test or scale will arrive at the same score.

The numbers on an instrument may be intended to be counters, nominal level of measurement, rank-order level, equal-interval, or ratio-level. The actual qualities or attributes being measured may or may not jibe with the level of measurement intended. The hope, however, is that they do.

If the scale is intended to measure physical attributes, often there can be agreement that ratio-level measurement has been attained. If, on the other hand, the attributes pertain to the human personality—such as a trait or an attitude—the scaled values are probably not more than rank-order, if that.

The procedure for devising psychometric scales is as follows:

1. An attribute is inferred to exist on suitably persuasive evidence. This "construct"—e.g., intelligence, trait, attitude, or other—is defined in at least general terms.
2. Next, a number of "signs" or indications representing the existence of the construct are chosen. If intelligence is the construct to be tested, an indicator may be based on the assumption that intelligence is signaled by knowledge of vocabulary. Thus an item calling for familiarity with a specific word might be chosen. A full set of such items is collected.
3. Finally, numbers are assigned to the chosen items by a rule of correspon-

dence that permits the numbers to indicate differing relationships between subjects responding to the items.

Although there are any number of rating scales, they can be broadly subsumed under three major classes: Likert-type, Thurstone-type, and Guttman-type.[10]
The Likert-type scale, also called the summated rating scale, or the equal-value scale, is distinguished because each item is considered to be of equal value. The subjects are asked to respond with agreement or disagreement to each item. The scores, then, are simply added up.

Thurstone-type scales, also called equal-appearing scales, present items that appear to be of equal value, but actually they have previously been assigned weighted values. Again, items checked off by the subject have their weighted values added together, for the total score.

Guttman-type scales, also called cumulative scales, presume that the items measure only one attribute variable on an ascending scale. The subjects are rated according to the amount of that attribute they possess.

Most researchers believe that the Likert-type scale is the easiest to construct and that it is as reliable—or more so—than the other two. Of course, any newly constructed scale must be "validated" by testing it on a standard group or sample before its results can be deemed generalizable to any other group.

There are countless modifications of these scales, each trying to avoid the errors implicit in all such scaling methods. The weakness in logical basis is blatant. Nevertheless, much material has been obtained that has been considered both practical and useful. Basic assumptions, however, must never be overlooked in evaluating scores; failure to be sensitive to the great possibility of error has caused much harm to individuals. From time to time, the news media reveal stories of children who have been mistakenly scored as retarded and thus deprived of proper care and schooling, and have even been institutionalized without justification.

The errors in criminal justice operations have not been so openly exploited in the news media, except perhaps the recent wave of judicial decisions decrying the lack of validity of entrance and promotion examinations in civil service.

One pervading error that has been sought to be remedied is the "response-set," or the tendency of some subject-respondents to be biased toward either agreement or disagreement with the perceived research objective. Thus the modification known as the forced-choice scales has been instituted, to try to match the discrimination and preference values of items, pair them, and insist that the subject make a choice between them. Unfortunately, however, the forced-choice scales become very large and complex, thus taxing the subjects' patience and endurance, and often losing their cooperation. Frequently neither of the choices offered is acceptable: "Do you admire or detest police officers?" may not provide reasonable alternatives to the subject.

To avoid that no-fair-choice dilemma, some researchers prefer the category rating scale, which offers several categories. The respondent chooses the one that he thinks best characterizes the attribute being rated, e.g., very good, good, no opinion, bad, or very bad.

To extend the possibility of analysis, the Category Rating Scale values are often given numbers. Such scales, called numerical rating scales, assume that the subject may equate the numbers with equal-interval subjective values, thus justifying the researcher's use of analytic techniques relying on this level of measurement.

Graphic rating scales present the subject with lines, bars, rectangles or other areas, with corresponding descriptive phrases, such as "most," "some," "little," or "least." The imagination of the draftsman is the only limit to this type, which assumes that people receive clearer impressions from the graphics, and therefore are more likely to respond in a way that is more truly representative of their subjective reaction.

In view of all the logical and theoretical obstacles, all research specialists consider scale construction to be a highly technical process, because it takes skill to reach for control of unwanted variance. In addition to the error of the response-set, there is also the possibility of a "halo effect," where a general impression will bias the response to individual items, and of personal biases toward either leniency or severity as the respondent sees proper role performance for himself.

The criminal justice professional is well advised to look for the frank revelation of all limitations, and for the frame of reference within which the results can be treated as approaching the necessary degree of validity for the intended use. The questioning of validity is a necessary task of all consumers of research findings and recommendations—whether research in the field or research reports of work performed elsewhere. Does it measure what it purports to measure? Does it measure what the researcher is interested in? Is what he is interested in really the thing he is seeking? In other words, is it valid?

"Reliability," when used to describe a measure in a research paper, may mean any of several different things, depending on the way it is conceived. Generally, it means the degree of consistency of scores on retest. "Precision" is usually defined as the variance of a sample distribution, or the spread between sequenced measures of the same item.

A final word on scales: Be skeptical of the validity of the basic assumptions, but use them when they are useful.[11]

Errors in Data Collection

The sources of error are manifold, and a separate work would be required even to cite the ways each data-collection technique is susceptible to its own unique pattern of error. It is possible, however, to classify the major types of errors.[12]

Measurement errors. Tools, scales, or units of measurement may be improper, or may change during the course of the inquiry. Also, human observers become more expert, fatigued, or inattentive as the research proceeds. Any of these occurrences would change the measurements in unpredictable degrees. Additionally, the subject(s) being measured may be changed by the act of measurement.

Time errors. Living samples change with time: they age, mature, or become ill or ill-disposed. Material objects decay, rust, or break down.

Biased samples. Any procedure other than true random sampling is subject to bias in initial selection. A differential dropping out of subjects between the beginning and the end of the inquiry also implies bias, as does self-selection by subjects.

Reaction and interaction. Subjects may react to the experimental or treatment situation, producing such phenomena as was noted in the famous Hawthorne study, where morale, group identification, and reevaluation of the subjects' response to A-treatment influence tended to produce either more or less B consequences.[13]

Statistical regression. Both high and low scores often contain summed errors that tend to exaggerate their difference. On retest, these errors may be redistributed, and the scores will regress to a more central value.

5 Data Analysis: Descriptive

There aren's twelve hundred people in the world who understand pictures. The others pretend and don't care.

Rudyard Kipling
The Light that Failed, Chap. 7

Cooperative Analysis

Analysis really starts before any actual data is collected. Often at the very inception of the research—certainly at the time the research design is formulated—consideration must be given to what analytical methods will be used for the data collected. These considerations will affect not only what data will be considered, but also in what form it should be collected. Without taking precautions in advance, a researcher can waste enormous effort collecting unanalyzable data.

If the researcher has insufficient computer programming, mathematical, statistical, or logical expertise, he should consult with qualified people in those fields. The advice of these analysts may modify the approach entirely so as to provide data in the form they will require for proper analysis.

The Importance of Level of Measurement[1]

One of the basic factors that will be considered by the mathematician or statistician is the level of measurement of the data that is proposed to be collected. The level is important because the statistical indexes proposed may not be useful for the particular scale measurement contemplated.

The use of analytical methods that assume equal-interval measurement when the data are actually ordinal or lower-level, is justified by some statisticians on grounds of expediency. The conservative approach, however, is to use only analytical procedures that assume no more than the data can completely justify as to level of measurement and degree of precision. When this rule is violated, there should be an open avowal, with the reasons stated in full to document the matter.

Data Management

If the observations have been few, it should be easy to comprehend their implications as data. It is easy to extract the "range," which is often the first manipulation to be performed because it gives an immediate perception of the general thrust of the massed figures (see the glossary).

Does the most frequent figure stand out clearly? If the numbers involved represent an interval or ratio scale (see the glossary), it would be permissible to add them all up and divide by the number of such values to obtain the arithmetic mean. This could be a valuable symbol of the data's "central tendency," as a summary index. It will be easy to grasp the form of the data when the observations are few. It may not be so easy to penetrate to the deeper implications of the figures.

For example, suppose the five police officers who attained the highest marks on the entrance examination studied for promotion. Two years later they were awarded the highest marks on the sergeants' examination. One year after that, however, every one of these five officers had left the department. In this case the data are few and easy to comprehend, but there isn't enough information to draw a valid conclusion. The conclusions one may draw from such a small quantity of information might go in any direction, depending on the examiner's prior experience or bias. On the basis of the data, about all one could really be sure of would be that more information is needed.

Usually, much more information is required to illuminate the dark crannies of problem areas. More details, more elements, more relationships, and so forth. In the study of criminal justice problems a researcher inevitably is led into collecting much data: dozens, hundreds, even thousands of numerical facts.

The difficulties with a paucity of information are reversed: huge masses of data to the uninitiated eye appear to be disorganized confusion—patterns are invisible because of the great amount of facts, especially today, when improved data-collecting methods culminate in an information explosion.

Techniques have been devised to handle massed data, to help discern the patterns. Most of these techniques can be subsumed under the term "descriptive statistics." Putting the figures into the form of a picture—a type of model—is often the easiest way to find useful patterns. (It must be remembered, however, that just as the arithmetic mean is a summary that may be useful in showing the central tendency of a group of data, it does not necessarily show the correct value for any single datum.)

Data-pictures of numbers are called graphics. Most large computers are now programmed to make such graphics—that is, they can find certain patterns in data and present them graphically.

Routinization

When any data-management scheme is developed ad hoc, with a view only to a specific ongoing research project, there are bound to be any number of bugs in the system. Errors are epidemic in research, and the contagion does not overlook analysis.

Whether the analysis involved is manual or computerized—of whatever degree—error comes unannounced. One systematic cure is to routinize all procedures, mechanizing whenever possible and reducing all procedures to the human equivalent of mechanization when that is all that can be done.

Since investigations are the very business of criminal justice workers, they usually think it is reasonable to demand routinization at every stage in data management. Even the routinization procedures themselves should be routinized.

Pseudoscientists and unqualified persons sometimes resist rigorous routinization of data management. Frequently they say they want to "keep their options open"—in other words, they're saying, "Throw the dice, and then I'll tell you how I'll bet." This is a mistake in the inception, and it leads to accidental or intentional errors. Loose data management violates the basic probabilistic principles of scientific inquiry.

The absolute necessity for routine procedures is brought into clear focus when research is considered as basically a search. Continuous research is undertaken in some aspect thousands of times a day. The National Crime Information Centers receive and process over 200,000 queries daily, many of them taking only seconds to complete. Without routinization of the searches, on-line demand service such as this would be impossible. It is essential that all aspects of data collection and analysis be made over into repetitive patterns of simple actions: routinized. As much as possible, it should be mechanized to eliminate the vagrant variance of human performance. Masses of data from ten to several hundred or thousands of elements are constantly being scanned for such patterns as frequency distributions, central tendency, and dispersion.

Manual handling of all these tasks introduces countless opportunities for untraceable error, and it takes so long that the results often are not available until much of the utility of the findings has been dissipated. For research to be optimally useful, faster results are needed.

The computer, developed to handle huge quantities of data, is well adapted to dealing with this problem in a mechanical, routine way.[2] The need for computerized data analysis is easily substantiated, simply because of the volume of data being analyzed in the United States alone. Also, by using remote terminals, a local agency can participate in its state's larger analytic resources. It is wasteful of the enormous national investment in computer hardware to use these powerful machines merely for remote filing and retrieval.

Flexible, on-line remote terminals permit even the smallest justice organization to participate in the services of a large regional computer, not only for automated filing, but also for analytical resources.

Under today's conditions there is no substitute for the computer in routinization of data management and analysis. The professional, while not expected to become a computer scientist, must learn the language involved, as a part of the larger communication problems in research. Also, criminal justice agencies must adopt methods of data handling that interface with computer requirements in order to use their facilities fully.

Massed Data

Data management requires the utmost precision in mathematical and statistical procedures. Further, provisions must be made to handle huge quantities of data. Finally, the results are needed quickly, in time to affect current operations.

Of these three criteria it appears that the time dimension is the most critical. However large the data base, and however precise, too late is too bad. Results are needed in "real time" so they can be used before conditions change.

With these conditions to be met in data handling, attention must be given to the analytical tools proposed in the research design. The respective virtues in each case—manual analysis, calculator, small computer, large computer in either batch or conversational modes—must be weighed. In almost every case, participation with other users in a large computer's analytical power will prove to be most advantageous, as long as the computer is used within a reasonably close percentage of its capacity. The large computer permits the degree of mechanization and routinization of procedures that returns the quickest results.

As long as the computer is not vastly underutilized, the costs should be comparable, or cheaper than, any other method.

Using Electronic Computers

The computer does not eliminate errors. On the contrary, in some respects errors become more of a menace. No computer hardware can operate without the software programming that directs its operations. It comes as a surprise to most people that software will often be more expensive than hardware in a computerized analytical system.

Software must be constantly updated to meet new needs and approaches. Further, it can take months to develop a large new program. It is an utter waste of time and effort to write a fresh program each time a procedure is to be used. Despite this, although many organizations have access to sophisticated hardware, for the most part the supporting software is at a far lower level. Often not much more than an automated file system is available, due mainly to the inadequacy of the software. A new planning framework is needed for criminal justice computer use. Research is often performed by technicians who are qualified in general terms but do not have experience in the particular task they are doing, or with the current type of equipment.

The design of all analysis must be reviewed by another analyst at least once. Unfortunately, this review is rarely done effectively. It is only later, after all the work is completed and the research effort is closed out, that complaints reveal that the analysis has failed in one or more respects.

To avoid this disaster, every effort should be made to critique the entire research design early enough to verify all proposed procedures, including data collection and presentation proposals. Everything should be fully documented in chronological order.

Criminal justice professionals do not have the time and training to serve as statisticians and computer specialists. As sophisticated as the social scientist may be in research, it is likely that he too will require the aid of both statistician and computer specialist. Even if he feels qualified, his research design proposals should be reviewed by specialists in each aspect of the design, especially concerning the proposed analytical methods.

Specialists, when giving their candid opinion, will point out the great savings involved in using "packaged programs" that are written with a view to scientific research and documented well enough to permit relatively untrained users to obtain all the basic descriptive indexes and graphics for investigative inquiry.

There are a number of such packaged programs well adapted to use by criminal justice people after minimum instruction. Most large computers are programmed for them, and all that is required to obtain their benefits is to buy the texts that give the syntactical rules, and to practice obtaining the correct results. Even for the neophyte user, they offer the hope of fewer mistakes than manual analysis.[3]

Unhappily, the statistical packaged programs most in use—such as BMD, DATA TEXT, STATJOB, and SPSS—are operable only in batch mode. Batch mode means that the program drives the computer via a completed deck of punched cards or other program code set up before being input to the computer. Any errors or "bugs" in the program are not revealed until the entire program is processed. Upon retrieval, the frequent incidence of flaws in the program as keypunched involves an exasperating amount of time and effort taken away from the examination of the information. It is not unusual to have keypunching error rates of over 10 percent.

The use of a remote terminal for small jobs, with retrieval and printing directly on the terminal, avoids some of the delay and expedites debugging, but it is no substitute for a true conversational mode. Fortunately, these programs are constantly being rewritten, and conversational versions of some of the packaged programs are being developed.

In conversational mode, or by using a program language such as BASIC that is adapted to interaction with the computer, the user can type in queries and obtain immediate response in print or on a visual display indicator. The immediacy of the computer's response permits the correction of all errors in minimal time, and adds greatly to the efficient, flexible use of the hardware's potential.

Analytic Procedures

How Much Data Have Been Collected?

The first question the analyst must consider is the quantity of information that is to be produced or has already been produced. Very small amounts may be handled best manually or perhaps with a minicomputer, or a simple calculator, not warranting the use of a large computer's time or facilities. Today arithmetic means, standard deviations, and other mathematical indexes are obtainable with a pocket calculator. The inconvenience involved in preparing the data for the large computer and getting it into the system may not be warranted. (Often the preparation of a small graph from few data may be done quickly by hand, at least in draft form, and it will be sufficient.)

When the data involves several hundred or more figures, manual manipulation becomes tedious, and when the data mass reaches thousands of values, it becomes utterly foolish to attempt to comprehend the group without computer assistance.

Getting the Picture

The maximum of information resides in the unrefined raw data. Any manipulation will at best ignore or blur some of the information in the data, or at worst, distort it. Nevertheless, there are many ways to describe gouped data that make it easier to see the implications involved.

In most research, the first task of analysis is to examine the distributional characteristics of each variable under investigation. For example, to find out something about the heights and weights of police officers, a researcher would measure them one by one, and obtain their heights, weights, and perhaps some additional information. The collected height-weight figures could look like the random listing on Figure 5-1, as printed out by an electronic computer.

The first listing, "71 170 2351," is printed from data input by an eighty-column data card, punched with those numbers. The first two vertical columns, "71," indicate the height of one officer in inches. The third column is blank to make the figures more legible (the machine does not require this). The fourth, fifth, and sixth columns, "170," are translated as the weight in pounds. The seventh column is blank, again only to make it more legible to the human reader. The eighth, ninth, tenth, and eleventh columns are codes for additional data.

The data were taken for each officer, as they happened to be encountered by the research assistant who measured them. While perhaps not truly a random order, the data are "unsorted."

Figure 5-2 shows the same data "sorted" by the machine in order of increasing heights and weights.

```
71 170 2351     70 161 2411     72 179 2541     73 181 1451
72 181 2641     68 153 2331     69 160 2451     83 211 2221
69 155 2341     70 168 2321     69 155 2431     71 171 2311
78 216 2451     72 185 1221     69 158 2321     71 180 4321
70 158 1451     77 225 2451     73 187 2551     71 165 2131
70 181 2451     69 156 3111     68 148 2341     77 201 3211
74 191 1451     75 190 4311     73 182 2451     71 169 2311
79 241 3331     76 200 2341     74 190 2541     70 162 2341
80 214 2221     74 197 2551     69 158 2351     69 160 5651
78 199 3331     77 199 2111     68 154 1111     75 195 1221
72 183 2441     78 219 2541     72 169 1222     76 208 2321
72 179 6561     70 172 3411     70 174 2341     70 162 2311
76 233 3231     68 158 2351     73 187 2351     70 173 1112
74 159 5551     71 179 1321     70 165 2351     73 273 2421
76 192 5551     68 149 2361     69 157 2311     68 151 1211
75 183 3321     71 175 5221     73 188 3251     71 178 1231
74 175 3331     76 201 2451     69 170 4331     72 180 2141
73 159 4441     73 190 2441     70 177 2441     68 163 2233
73 162 3331     70 161 2321     78 210 2321     73 181 2541
72 170 2221     71 203 1311     73 178 2251     70 171 2341
70 175 4441     70 172 2261     71 176 4311     70 168 1241
70 165 4231     70 158 2651     69 160 1322     77 215 2451
71 159 5551     70 168 3441     69 160 4561     68 149 2351
73 183 2221     68 141 1211     69 169 1322     70 164 2651
68 150 2331     75 198 1551     70 175 2541     78 207 2341
69 155 2221     78 202 2131     78 215 4221     74 199 2321
68 160 3331     69 159 2323     69 161 2311     75 194 4311
69 160 6521     75 199 2351     77 205 1451     70 202 2511
69 175 2351     68 138 2341     70 171 2321     68 142 2311
76 200 2451     70 169 4341     72 180 6551     71 174 3521
72 191 1451     71 171 3441     76 198 2321     68 156 2311
68 150 1332     70 178 2311     69 158 4351
75 196 6551     74 195 2351     70 160 2311
75 202 2621     71 200 2421     74 220 1312
69 154 2341     71 181 2321     70 162 2351
68 151 1311     72 167 2451     80 218 2451
72 183 2441     70 169 1331     68 149 2341
73 181 2331     68 150 1342     68 166 1321
70 170 2441     71 174 6641     78 205 2321
69 161 6661     75 195 2331     68 147 1322
72 182 4431     72 203 2541     70 169 2541
76 203 1541     69 165 2311     74 187 1231
70 176 2331     73 185 2331     76 197 1341
70 177 2241     70 171 1421     71 174 2131
70 170 3441     70 161 2551     68 152 1321
71 178 2321     70 171 2451     70 165 2411
69 160 1461     72 174 2431     72 184 2331
69 160 1312     70 175 2321     79 217 1541
76 205 2111     70 159 2652     76 192 2311
71 169 2441     71 177 5441     75 195 2351
73 185 2451     69 157 3321     74 192 2531
                70 159 1241     70 171 2451
                73 189 2551     68 172 1111
                69 164 2312     72 186 2331
                69 159 2311     72 172 1311
                72 172 2361     73 183 2351
                70 169 2411     73 189 1451
```

Figure 5-1. Random Data: Sample No. 1—Heights, Weights, and Other Data (196 Observations).

```
68 138 2341

68 141 1211        70 162 2311        72 174 2431        76 200 2341
68 142 2311        70 164 2651        72 179 2541        76 201 2451
68 147 1322        70 165 2411        72 179 6561        76 203 1541
68 148 2341        70 165 2351        72 180 6551        76 205 2111
68 149 2341        70 165 4231        72 180 2141        76 208 2321
68 149 2351        70 168 2321        72 181 2641        76 233 3231
68 149 2361        70 168 3441        72 182 4431        77 199 2111
68 150 1342        70 168 1241        72 183 2441        77 201 3211
68 150 1332        70 169 2411        72 183 2441        77 205 1451
68 150 2331        70 169 2541        72 184 2331        77 215 2451
68 151 1311        70 169 1331        72 185 1221        77 225 2451
68 151 1211        70 169 4341        72 186 2331        78 199 3331
68 152 1321        70 170 2441        72 191 1451        78 202 2131
68 153 2331        70 170 3441        72 203 2541        78 205 2321
68 154 1111        70 171 2321        73 159 4441        78 207 2341
68 156 2311        70 171 1421        73 162 3331        78 210 2321
68 158 2351        70 171 2451        73 178 2251        78 215 4221
68 160 3331        70 171 2341        73 181 1451        78 216 2451
68 163 2233        70 171 2451        73 181 2541        78 219 2541
68 166 1321        70 172 2261        73 181 2331        79 217 1541
68 172 1111        70 172 3411        73 182 2451        79 241 3331
69 154 2341        70 173 1112        73 183 2351        80 214 2221
69 155 2221        70 174 2341        73 183 2221        80 218 2451
69 155 2341        70 175 2321        73 185 2451        83 211 2221
69 155 2431        70 175 2541        73 185 2331
69 156 3111        70 175 4441        73 187 2551
69 157 2311        70 176 2331        73 187 2351
69 157 3321        70 177 2241        73 188 3251
69 158 2321        70 177 2441        73 189 2551
69 158 2351        70 178 2311        73 189 1451
69 158 4351        70 181 2451        73 190 2441
69 159 2311        70 202 2511        73 273 2421
69 159 2323        71 159 5551        74 159 5551
69 160 1312        71 165 2131        74 175 3331
69 160 1461        71 169 2311        74 187 1231
69 160 6521        71 169 2441        74 190 2541
69 160 2451        71 170 2351        74 191 1451
69 160 4561        71 171 3441        74 192 2531
69 160 1322        71 171 2311        74 195 2351
69 160 5651        71 174 3521        74 197 2551
69 161 2311        71 174 2131        74 199 2321
69 161 6661        71 174 6641        74 220 1312
69 164 2312        71 175 5221        75 183 3321
69 165 2311        71 176 4311        75 190 4311
69 169 1322        71 177 5441        75 194 4311
69 170 4331        71 178 1231        75 195 1221
69 175 2351        71 178 2321        75 195 2351
70 158 1451        71 179 1321        75 195 2331
70 158 2651        71 180 4321        75 196 6551
70 159 1241        71 181 2321        75 198 1551
70 159 2652        71 200 2421        75 199 2351
70 160 2311        71 203 1311        75 202 2621
70 161 2551        72 167 2451        76 192 5551
70 161 2321        72 169 1222        76 192 2311
70 161 2411        72 170 2221        76 197 1341
70 162 2351        72 172 2361        76 198 2321
70 162 2341        72 172 1311        76 200 2451
```

Figure 5-2. Sorted Data: Sample No. 1—Heights, Weights, and Other Data (196 Observations).

Histograms: Univariate Analysis

To discover how heights are distributed in a police force would be to study only *one* variable. Actually, height is a continuous variable, which in the previous discussion was marked off in equal intervals or values of 1 inch, starting at 68 inches. In scientific terms, a researcher would say, "I want to take each *value* of that variable, and count how many times it appears in the data."

The data could be sorted manually, of course, and it would be found that there are twenty-one occasions of 68 inches, twenty-five of 69 inches, and so on. The manual process is tedious and surprisingly susceptible to errors. The computer, however, does that job automatically and easily by selecting a "sort" packaged program. At the same time a sort is done, a graphic called a histogram can be printed out.

A sample histogram for height data appears in Figure 5-3. This printout is from a packaged program called STATJOB, run on a Univac 1106 at the Southeast Data Center at Florida International University. It shows characteristics peculiar to that particular packaged program. The criminal justice professional should become familiar with the pecularities of the printouts available because it is far too wasteful of time to have the printout done over by hand.

The histogram is a plot of the relationship between the magnitude of the observations and the number of the observations. It is customary to use the horizontal axis to scale off the magnitudes or values of the variable. The vertical axis is scaled off in appropriate counts, or "frequency" intervals.

A compromise between amount of effort and loss of information usually calls for not less than seven and not more than about twenty groupings of magnitude. Here the groupings amount to thirteen $[(80 - 68) + 1]$. The specific values are typed in at intervals of three as a peculiarity of the STATJOB system. (See the reproductions of the punched cards that constitute the "runstream" for this histogram and accompanying indexes in Appendix F.)

The columns of asterisks constitute the measure of the frequencies detected by the computer. Another peculiarity of this printout is that each asterisk does *not* represent one observation, unless the total frequency in that column is 40. If the frequency in the data is more than 40, the column will be foreshortened; if the frequency in the data is less than 40, the column will be heightened by a very small proportion. The histogram is for visual approximation, and this slight discrepancy with the data is not too harmful if it is recognized for what it is.

The columns of dashes next to each column of asterisks indicate the "normal" frequency that the data would have taken had it demonstrated a normal curve of the same number of observations. The normal curve is much flatter than the data curve, thus it is immediately apparent how the data differ from a normal distribution: more peaked around the middle, too high at the upper end.

The normal curve is the shape the data often take when they represent

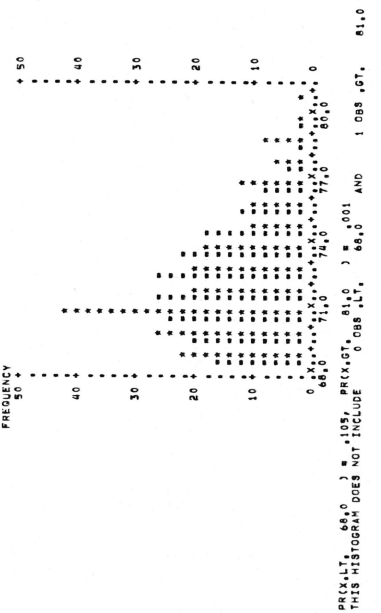

Figure 5-3. Histogram.

"natural" occurrences, such as dimensions of living organisms and errors of performance.

Experience from measuring hundreds of thousands of humans has indicated that in a homogeneous group, their heights will tend to group in a bell-shaped frequency curve. This has been a tremendous convenience, because a relatively simple mathematical formula can describe this normal curve and measure the area under it. Since in a frequency curve, the area under the curve represents the number of observations, a mathematician or a computer can easily compare an input of a number of observations, build the normal curve that could be expected from that number of observations and the range from those approximate values, and then compare that normal curve with the actual frequency curve of the data input. The normal curve is valuable because it provides a convenient and useful standard to use to compare, which is the basis of measurement.

The data curve does not yield the normally expected data frequencies. The notation under the histogram—PR(X.LT. 68.0) = .105, PR(X.GT. 81.0) = .001—gives more precise figures about the abnormality. The line is translated as follows: "If the population from which the sample was drawn is 'normal' in distribution, the probability (PR) of obtaining values "Less Than 68.0 is .105," or about 10 percent. And the "probability (PR) of obtaining values Greater Than 81.0 is .001," or about 0.1 percent. The information is presented very simply, yet very precisely.

The printout announces to all who can read it that this may not be a representative sample. *If* the population of heights from which it was drawn is, in fact, normally distributed, the sample is very unusual. To obtain a fair representation of the population, it is necessary to take more samples. If, as seems very possible, the sample is representative of the real population, the population is very biased in the direction of being much taller, for some unknown reason, than the "normal" population.

The latter situation happens to be true: The police department from which these data were taken has a minimum height requirement of 68 inches. Further, remeasurement revealed that there was an internal bias caused by the data collectors' tendency to agree with officers who protested at being marked as "short." The data collectors would agree with the subjects that they were taller than the actual value scale value measured. But they were reluctant to score 72 inches because that would be announcing that the officer was 6 feet.

Note that 71 inches is the score that seems most out of proportion to expected frequencies on the histogram shown in Figure 5-3. It appears that the observers would go along and add a little to the measure, or sympathetically— perhaps even unconsciously—"see it their way," but there were certain strong internalized limits. The comment from one of the collectors was, "There's no way those shorties are going to get marked up to 6 feet!" Thus the cold black-and-white printout provides clues to human interaction.

Indexes of Distribution

The histogram gives a general view of how the data frequencies arrange themselves, it creates order out of the chaos of the data as it is collected, and it provides some evidence upon which to base guesses (inferences) about the population itself.

There is literally no end to the number and kind of indexes that can be devised by statisticians to describe masses of data. A smaller number, however, have been found to be consistently useful. It is possible to "call" for some of the most frequently useful indices with the same packaged programs that yield histograms. In fact, at the same time it printed out the histogram shown in Figure 5-3, the program printed the indexes shown in Figure 5-4.

Distribution indexes are a set of summary numbers, each of which gives a partial description of the data.[4]

"Arithmetic mean" is the sum of the values of all the observations, divided by the number of observations. It is the most frequently used single index because it shows an unbiased estimate of the population-mean. That is, it shows the central tendency of the data clearly and simply. Note, however, that the value printed as .71776+02 should be read as 71.776. The +02 signifies that the decimal point should be moved two places to the right. The same convention, used for technical reasons, prevails down the list for all twelve indexes (from no. 2 through no. 13).

"Standard error of mean" is a measure of the stability of the arithmetic mean—that is, it estimates the potential degree of discrepancy between sample mean and the (usually) unknown population mean.

"Studentized mean" is the arithmetic mean divided by the standard error of the mean.

"Unbiased variance" is an unbiased estimate of the population variance about the mean. That is, it is an estimate that equals, on the average, the value of variance of the population. It is calculated as the average of the squared deviations from the sample mean; the glossary has the algebraic form.

"Standard deviation" is the square root of the unbiased variance; it measures the dispersion of the data values about the mean.

"Coefficient of variation" is the standard deviation divided by the arithmetic mean. This index measures the variability of the data values about the arithmetic mean. It is usually used only when all observations are of the same sign, as is the case here.

"Mean absolute deviation" is similar to the variance in reflecting variability; it is calculated as the average of the absolute deviations from the arithmetic mean.

"Minimum value" is, obviously, the lowest value of the observations.

"Maximum value" is the highest observation value.

```
S T A T I S T I C S    F O R    V A R I A B L E    1    HEIGHT
```

/1. NO. OF OBSERVATIONS...................   196

2. ARITHMETIC MEAN....................... .71776+02
3. STANDARD ERROR OF MEAN............... .21990+00
4. STUDENTIZED MEAN..................... .32640+03

5. UNBIASED VARIANCE.................... .94776+01
6. STANDARD DEVIATION................... .30786+01
7. COEFFICIENT OF VARIATION............. .42892-01
8. MEAN ABSOLUTE DEVIATION.............. .25031+01

9. MINIMUM VALUE........................ .68000+02
10. MAXIMUM VALUE........................ .83000+02
11. RANGE................................ .15000+02

12. COEFFICIENT OF SKEWNESS.............. .92455+00
13. COEFFICIENT OF KURTOSIS.............. .33004+01

14. NO. RUNS UP AND DOWN.................   112
15. P(112 OR FEWER RUNS UP AND DOWN).....   .00
16. P(112 OR MORE RUNS UP AND DOWN)......   1.00
17. LENGTH OF LONGEST RUN UP AND DOWN...   6
18. P(LONGEST RUN IS 6 OR LESS)........   .99
19. P(LONGEST RUN IS 6 OR MORE)........   .06

20. NO. RUNS ABOVE AND BELOW MEDIAN......   84
21. NO. OBSERVATIONS ABOVE MEDIAN........   86
22. NO. OBSERVATIONS BELOW MEDIAN........   90
23. P(84 OR FEWER RUNS ABOVE AND BELOW)   .25
24. P(84 OR MORE RUNS ABOVE AND BELOW).   .79

25. CONFIDENCE INT. FOR MEAN AT 95.0 % LEVEL   (.71342+02, .72209+02)
26. CONFIDENCE INT. FOR VARIANCE AT 95.0 % LEVEL (.78455+01, .11681+02)

27. PERCENTILES
        5%   25%   50%   75%   95%   TRI-MEAN
     .68000+02 .70000+02 .71000+02 .73000+02 .78000+02 .71250+02

Figure 5-4. Statistical Indexes.

"Range" is the maximum minus the minimum value.

"Coefficient of skewness" is a measure of the deviation of the curve from the symmetry on each side exhibited by the normal curve, which in this index has a value of zero. A positive value means that the distribution elongates to the right. A negative value means that the distribution elongates to the left. It is sometimes difficult to tell that the data are skewed by inspection of numbered data, which is why this index is valuable. There is another way to determine skewness: if the mean is drawn away from the median (the observation exactly in the middle), the data are skewed in the direction of the mean.

"Coefficient of kurtosis" is a measure of the relative peakedness or flatness of the curve. A normal distribution will have a coefficient of 3. for this version (STATPACK). Larger values indicate a flatter distribution than normal.

The most used of the above indexes are the mean, maximum, minimum, and range indexes. A useful index, though not quite so often seen, is "percentiles," which measures the variable at various points on the scale, from the place where 5 percent of the values have been listed, to 25 percent, and so on. Another useful though relatively unused index is the "tri-mean," which is a weighted average of the 25-percent, 50-percent, and 75-percent percentiles. This index avoids the weakness of the arithmetic mean, which tends to respond too easily to extreme values at either end.

Another index, the fiftieth percentile (see no. 27 in Figure 5-4), which avoids the weakness of the mean is the "median." The fiftieth percentile is the value exactly in the middle when the number of observations is odd; it is the average of the two on each side of the missing middle when the number of observations is even. It is easily obtained by inspecting the histogram or a "sort" of the values in order of magnitude.

The mode is another frequently used index, although it does not describe the bulk of the data very well. The mode is the observation with the largest "count" or frequency, which is easily picked out from the histogram as 71.0 inches.

The indexes commonly called the "central tendency" indexes are the arithmetic mean, median, and mode. The "studentized mean," however, is certainly just as much an index of central tendency. It is not so frequently used, though it has certain advantages in estimating the population because it contains in one index an estimate of the population mean, with an allowance for discrepancy.

The most commonly used indexes of "dispersion" about the mean are the unbiased variance and the standard deviation. The standard deviation is extremely important to those who are interested in doing statistical manipulations.

Verifying the Statistics

The next set of indexes, from no. 14 through no. 24 in Figure 5-4, is useful in determining whether the input sequence of the data is random. Very large or very small probabilities could be a signal to the researcher of a lack of randomness in the presentation of the data. This has a number of easily imagined uses, not the least of which is a check on the activities of the data collectors.

The "confidence interval for mean" shows the probability that the printed mean-interval values contain the unknown population mean. Even if the data are not normally distributed, the basic assumption of this index does not provide much restriction.

The "confidence interval for variance" tries to measure the probability that the printed values contain the unknown population variance. However, the assumption that the observations have a normal distribution is a bit critical. Should the data distribution not be at least approximately normal, this confidence interval could be incorrect.

The "percentiles" index has been discussed in part above. The values are useful to indicate the form of the distribution. The fiftieth percentile is also known as the median.

Cross-Tabulations and Graphs: Bivariate Analysis

Most of the indexes listed in Figure 5-4 assume that the data are interval or higher scale. What would happen if the data are merely ordinal or nominal in scale, that is, nonquantitative? Such an example would be hair color.

The different hair colors could be tabled in a frequency count. They could even be cross-tabulated against other variables, as done in Chapter 2. If there is a great quantity of data, the computer is a time-saver for cross-tabulation, too.

In fact, the computer can be used to cross-tabulate two variables at a time, such as heights and weights. Even if there is a third variable, most packaged programs will tabulate in a series of bivariate tables. Thus if height, weight, and color were to be cross-tabulated, a computer could print out a tabulation of height against weight; height against color; and weight against hair color. Each one of these tabulations would be a bivariate analysis, showing the relationships between two variables—if *A* then *B*.

The difference between a crossbreak and a cross-tabulation as used in this book is that a crossbreak is a partitioning of an entire population. A cross-tabulation is the more general tabular presentation of any kind, without any requirement that an entire population be partitioned.

For simplicity, the earlier discussions of breaks did not include in the cells any indication of the percentage of the population that the total figure indicated. This can be a very useful piece of data, and it should almost invariably be included. A computer can calculate these percentages easily and rapidly; in fact, most packaged programs that cross-tabulate will automatically include the percentage figures. An example is the computer printout of the bivariate crosstabulation for heights and weights of the patrolmen for the data presented (Figure 5-5).

Note that this is a 13 × 12 cross-tabulation. The vertical "rows" are read first, then the horizontal "columns."

If a cell is to be pointed out, it is identified by the row, then the column

ROWS.......CATEGORIES OF HEIGHT
COLUMNS.....CATEGORIES OF WEIGHT

	140 TO 150-	150 TO 160-	160 TO 170-	170 TO 180-	180 TO 190-	190 TO 200-	200 TO 210-
68 TO 69-	7 / 3.59	10 / 5.13	3 / 1.54	1 / .51	0 / .00	0 / .00	0 / .00
69 TO 70-	0 / .00	12 / 6.15	12 / 6.15	2 / 1.03	0 / .00	0 / .00	0 / .00
70 TO 71-	0 / .00	4 / 2.05	18 / 9.23	18 / 9.23	1 / .51	0 / .00	1 / .51
71 TO 72-	0 / .00	1 / .51	3 / 1.54	12 / 6.15	2 / 1.03	0 / .00	2 / 1.03
72 TO 73-	0 / .00	0 / .00	2 / 1.03	6 / 3.08	9 / 4.62	1 / .51	1 / .51
73 TO 74-	0 / .00	1 / .51	1 / .51	1 / .51	13 / 6.67	1 / .51	0 / .00
74 TO 75-	0 / .00	1 / .51	0 / .00	1 / .51	1 / .51	6 / 3.08	0 / .00
75 TO 76-	0 / .00	0 / .00	0 / .00	0 / .00	1 / .51	8 / 4.10	1 / .51
76 TO 77-	0 / .00	0 / .00	0 / .00	0 / .00	0 / .00	4 / 2.05	6 / 3.08
77 TO 78-	0 / .00	0 / .00	0 / .00	0 / .00	0 / .00	1 / .51	2 / 1.03
78 TO 79-	0 / .00	0 / .00	0 / .00	0 / .00	0 / .00	1 / .51	3 / 1.54
79 TO 80-	0 / .00	0 / .00	0 / .00	0 / .00	0 / .00	0 / .00	0 / .00
80 AND GREATER	0 / .00	0 / .00	0 / .00	0 / .00	0 / .00	0 / .00	0 / .00
TOTAL	7 / 3.59	29 / 14.87	39 / 20.00	41 / 21.03	27 / 13.85	22 / 11.28	16 / 8.21

BIVARIATE STATISTICS FOR COUNTS
CHI-SQUARE (WITH CONT. CORR.) = 402.04 WITH 132 DF
THE NORMALIZED CHI-SQUARE = 16.62
PHI = 1.44   CONTINGENCY COEF = .82
KENDALL'S S = 12689,   STANDARDIZED S = 14.236
TAU-C = .73   DCR = .75

Figure 5-5. Cross-tabulation.

81

```
        *          *          *          *          *
 210 TO * 220 TO * 230 TO * 240 TO *250 AND *
  220=  *  230=  *  240=  *  250=  *GREATER *  TOTAL
**********************************************************
        *          *          *          *          *
   0 *      0 *      0 *      0 *      0 *     21      COUNT
 .00 *    .00 *    .00 *    .00 *    .00 *  10.77      PPLANE
**********************************************************
        *          *          *          *          *
   0 *      0 *      0 *      0 *      0 *     26      COUNT
 .00 *    .00 *    .00 *    .00 *    .00 *  13.33      PPLANE
**********************************************************
        *          *          *          *          *
   0 *      0 *      0 *      0 *      0 *     42      COUNT
 .00 *    .00 *    .00 *    .00 *    .00 *  21.54      PPLANE
**********************************************************
        *          *          *          *          *
   0 *      0 *      0 *      0 *      0 *     20      COUNT
 .00 *    .00 *    .00 *    .00 *    .00 *  10.26      PPLANE
**********************************************************
        *          *          *          *          *
   0 *      0 *      0 *      0 *      0 *     19      COUNT
 .00 *    .00 *    .00 *    .00 *    .00 *   9.74      PPLANE
**********************************************************
        *          *          *          *          *
   0 *      0 *      0 *      0 *      1 *     18      COUNT
 .00 *    .00 *    .00 *    .00 *    .51 *   9.23      PPLANE
**********************************************************
        *          *          *          *          *
   0 *      1 *      0 *      0 *      0 *     10      COUNT
 .00 *    .51 *    .00 *    .00 *    .00 *   5.13      PPLANE
**********************************************************
        *          *          *          *          *
   0 *      0 *      0 *      0 *      0 *     10      COUNT
 .00 *    .00 *    .00 *    .00 *    .00 *   5.13      PPLANE
**********************************************************
        *          *          *          *          *
   0 *      0 *      1 *      0 *      0 *     11      COUNT
 .00 *    .00 *    .51 *    .00 *    .00 *   5.64      PPLANE
**********************************************************
        *          *          *          *          *
   1 *      1 *      0 *      0 *      0 *      5      COUNT
 .51 *    .51 *    .00 *    .00 *    .00 *   2.56      PPLANE
**********************************************************
        *          *          *          *          *
   4 *      0 *      0 *      0 *      0 *      8      COUNT
2.05 *    .00 *    .00 *    .00 *    .00 *   4.10      PPLANE
**********************************************************
        *          *          *          *          *
   1 *      0 *      0 *      1 *      0 *      2      COUNT
 .51 *    .00 *    .00 *    .51 *    .00 *   1.03      PPLANE
**********************************************************
        *          *          *          *          *
   3 *      0 *      0 *      0 *      0 *      3      COUNT
1.54 *    .00 *    .00 *    .00 *    .00 *   1.54      PPLANE
**********************************************************
        *          *          *          *          *
   9 *      2 *      1 *      1 *      1 *    195      COUNT
4.62 *   1.03 *    .51 *    .51 *    .51 * 100.00      PPLANE


     PROB( CHI=SQUARE .GT.   402.04 ) =    .0000
     CRAMER'S V =      .43

     DRC          =      .78
```

Figure 5-5. (cont.)

number starting at the upper left-hand corner. Thus cell 3,4 shows twenty officers were "70-71" and "170-180," and those eighteen officers constituted 9.23 percent of the entire sample, which is given as 196. If a data card had mistakenly been punched with values not within the scales, it would have been rejected, and the sample size would have been reduced by one. Thus the cross-tabulation shows how many times a given height "went with" a given weight.

Cross-tabulations can be fascinating because they give precise figures, with all the patterns of relationships laid out numerically. When there are huge quantities of data, however, they can be overwhelming. Nevertheless, it is necessary to learn to read cross-tabulations easily and fluently to be able to critique a research report and make good sense out of it.

(The "bivariate statistics for counts" list at the bottom of Figure 5-5 shows a series of indexes giving numerical values to relationships, which will be discussed in the next chapter.)

Another graphic the computer can print out is the scattergram, a plot of the values of the cross-tabulation. Two values, variably corresponding with each other, can be graphed to show the bivariate relationship at a glance (Figure 5-6).

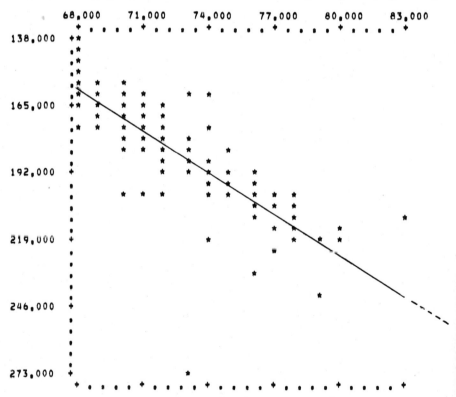

Figure 5-6. Scattergram.

Ordinarily, the horizontal (x) axis is scaled for the independent (A) variable. The vertical (y) axis is scaled for the dependent (B) variable.

Although different analyses could reverse the sequence, consider here that *height* is the independent variable, and that the *weight* variable is "dependent" on it.

Because there are so many "strikeovers" of identical locations, it is possible to get only a general idea of how strongly the values "regress" to a specific line. The cross-tabulation can be consulted for any specific information about that. Another alternative is to calculate and ink in the regression line, which is what was done in the figure. Yet another alternative is to use another program that will ink in the regression line by machine.

One peculiarity of this printout of the scattergram is that the low values for the horizontal scale are on the left-hand side as usual, but they are printed at the *top* of the graph. Also, the low values for the vertical scale are at the *top* of that scale, instead of at the bottom. This is the case because it is much easier and faster for the machine to print out in this manner, rather than from bottom to top, as is usual. The accuracy is not affected, but one must take care to note this peculiarity of this packaged program's printout.

It is interesting to see how the regression line seductively leads toward prediction. If the height of the officer is known, there is a lot of information about what his weight is likely to be. The line gives the basis for rational inference, not only about the members of the sample, but also about the larger population from which it has been drawn, and about other samples that might be drawn. That subject will be considered in the following chapter.

Transforming Scores

As observations are written in the form necessary for the type of data and procedures set up, they are called "raw scores." These raw scores do not tell much until they are compared with scores of a standard group. Often it is necessary to transform the observed raw scores into "derived" scores to facilitate this comparison with a standard.[5]

There is no limit to the number of systems that can be devised for transforming scores to make such comparisons. As mentioned previously, a derived score is customary in intelligence testing to permit the comparison of children of different ages. The raw score of the intelligence test is divided by the age of the child to give a derived score that is called an intelligence quotient.

It is known that ten-year-old children exhibit more absolute ability, and presumably more absolute intelligence, than eight-year old children. The derived score, the intelligence quotient (IQ), is used to predict ultimate intellectual ability, by estimating current potential. The comparison of IQs permits measuring one group of children's potential with another group of a different size and of a different age.

Finding the relative standing of two officers, one attaining nineteenth position in a West Point class of 600 and the other assigned nineteenth position in a college class of 20, is one of many similar problems calling for a comparison of relative class standings of values that are members of different-sized groups.

There are a number of ways to obtain derived scores that will make their relationship instantly comprehensible. One way is to determine their respective percentile ranks. Thus the officer who is nineteenth in a class of 600 is 582/600 along the range from the lowest student, and is therefore in the ninety-seventh percentile range. The college student who was nineteenth in a class of 20 is second above the lowest, or in the tenth percentile.

Another derived score that provides a standard of comparison of rankings in different sized groups—and does a bit more than that—is the Z-score, also called "standard score" because it is merely the number of standard deviations the raw score is distant from the mean of the distribution of which it is a part.

In Figure 5-4, the standard deviation was given in the same units as the raw score—in that case, inches of height. Each raw score, given in inches of height, is so many inches from the mean of that group. That figure divided by the value of the standard deviation is the Z-score.

The reasoning behind the standard-score transformation is quite straightforward. Frequently, scores of a group of data will arrange themselves about an arithmetic mean, which is often the best single indicator of the group's central tendency. The amount of dispersion about that mean is another distinguishing characteristic of a group. Thus these two characteristics together form the standard deviation index.

Among other things, measures of dispersion constitute bases for estimating errors in prediction. If the population is normally distributed, the sample mean is probably the best single predictor of the population mean. The standard deviation measures the dispersion of values from the mean, so that the variability of different distributions can be compared in terms of the standard deviation.

For example, imagine a sample p of population P, and a sample q of population Q. In each case the mean of the respective samples would be the best guess (inference) as to the mean of the appropriate population. But if sample p has a larger standard deviation than sample q, the guess about population P is more likely to be in error.

The standard deviation also permits precise interpretation of values within a given distribution. For a single score to be interpreted, it must be compared with a collection of scores from some reference group. For example, the information that a Watusi policeman is 6 feet tall might be impressive. However, given the information that the reference group of all Watusi policemen has an arithmetic mean of 6 feet, 6 inches, the 6-foot officer is rather short in comparison. On the contrary, in Japan, a policeman who is 5 feet, 5 inches tall might be rather tall compared to his reference group.

Z-scores change all values to units of the standard deviation of *that* group, thus giving an appreciation of how that score relates to the average of that group. A Z-score of $+1$ means that score is one standard deviation away from the mean, on the high end of the scale. A Z-score of -2 means that the value lies two standard deviations lower than the arithmetic mean of that group.

A Z-score of -2 from another group means exactly the same thing about its own group. Both officers would be among the shortest 2.28 percent of officers. Stated another way, 97.72 percent of policemen in their respective groups, of whatever size, would be taller than they, even though one or both may be 6 feet tall or taller.

Another score the criminal justice professional may encounter in research reports is the T-score, which is merely a transformation of Z-scores to eliminate the negative numbers, which are so inconvenient in mass computation.

All the above measures, indexes, and scores provide shorthand descriptions that facilitate the comprehension of mass data. Comparatively simple to understand and use, they are constantly cited in research reports. They can be computed with electronic assistance at the push of a button. All professionals in criminal justice should become familiar with them so that they can read and instantly grasp the implications and relevance of these figures when they see them in reports. They should also be able to come to their own decisions as to the measures' pertinence, validity, and how far the measures violate basic assumptions of the data to which they are applied.

True, professionals may seek advice in difficult cases from statisticians. Inasmuch that statistics is as much art as science, however, they must be responsible for the final decision.

It is rare that there is not one or more violations of basic assumptions in the average research report. If the possibility of error is known and the risk is taken because some approximate information is more helpful to decision-making than none at all, there may be no objection. An administrator, however, cannot afford to take *unknowing* risks. There is considerable evidence that the public is ready to accept statements of probability of success regarding proposed projects or remedial programs. Administration is showing increasing acceptance of innovation in social projects. The reality of the case is that many of the efforts will not succeed.

Mere proclamation of achievement can no longer suffice to guarantee administrative survival. Claims of victory very often have been proved to be without substance. An experimental stance toward creative approaches and operational change seems to be the modern manager's necessary armament. Thus clear statements of the *probabilities* regarding proposed actions should be made. For example, "This project appears to have a probability of partial success, amounting to 50 percent, and a low probability of complete success of about 10 percent. Complete success would save about $350,000.00. Partial success should show savings of about $20,000.00."

6

Data Analysis: Inferential

The power to guess the unseen from the seen . . .

Henry James
The Art of Fiction

Inferential Analysis

Inference from Observations

The data have been collected and descriptively analyzed, and the patterns concealed within the mass have been revealed by graphics and indexes. What can be inferred from the data and these model summaries?[1] Particularly, what can be reliably inferred in relation to the if-*A*-then-*B* statement?

The attempt to answer that question shows why the analyst should participate in the origins of the research design. Ultimately, analysis is his problem. His response will depend on the detailed procedures of the research, and the procedures used may have forestalled possibility of any valid analysis.

To phrase the question more generally: What can be inferred from *any* observation? The answer must be that it depends.

The factors appear to be manifold. Some matters can be inferred because additional information is hidden from notice within the known data. Other matters might indicate a trend over time, which points a way toward inferring the future that is unknowable as a certainty, but calculable as a probability.

A Posteriori Probability

If long observation indicates that a certain event occurs 90 percent of the time, and the event being researched resembles in all known ways the prior event, a researcher often anticipates the probability that the event will reoccur about 90 percent of the time.

A Prior Probability

Another probable calculation would be used if there are, say, 100 known ways an event can turn out, and 85 of those events are favorable to the cause. The probability might be estimated as 85 percent, *if* both the favorable and unfavorable events are equally likely. The odds of throwing a seven on the first throw of the dice are six out of a possible thirty-six arrangements of the two cubes—one chance out of six.

"Markers" are invariably (or almost so) associated with predictable events, and one often reaches for a judgment based on the incidence of such markers. This method was used to estimate the likelihood that certain of the Federalist Papers were written by Madison, rather than Hamilton, based on Madison's known prediliction for the word "whilst," and Hamilton's avoidance of the word.[2]

Other approaches have been called "personal probability," and Bayesian inference.[3] There is no real need for the criminal justice professional to become versed in the remote reaches of this, or any of the other technical provinces with which he interfaces. It suffices to know that the level at which even behavioral scientists conceive of probability is far from the last word on the subject.[4] Theoretical statisticians and mathematicians differ in their interpretation of probability statements. The criminal justice professional should retain the attitude of a judge or juror, and request to be shown justification for all methods, and compare the positions taken with alternatives offered by other equally qualified experts.

Inference About the Past or Present State of Facts

Criminal justice investigations often use observation as the source of data. A detective may observe someone peering into parked cars, trying the handles. Does that permit him to infer that the person is about to commit larceny?

Does the fact that a youth "sneaks" out of an alley at 3:00 A.M., wearing a short jacket and soft, rubber-soled shoes indicate that he has burglarized a building back there? Can the detective infer the construct of burglary?

The basic weakness of such data for inferential purposes is that it is incomplete. The detective must provide additional correct data input from his long experience with criminal behavior, or else he is quite likely to make wrong inferences from his observations. Important data in criminal justice require a deep understanding and knowledge of the *meaning* of deviant and organizational behavior to permit valid inferences.

In all research, observer-inference is plagued with difficulties. Personal bias and human error of observation are only some of them. Often the mere presence of the observer changes the situation that is being observed. In addition, there are data-blanks caused by restricted fields of observation.

Information about past or present events calls for a human judgment adapted to the situation. There is no known mathematical procedure for ascertaining causality. Scientists say they are looking for a "relationship," a "correspondence," or "one element producing another." Mathematicians say, "one variable is a function of another," for example, $y = f(x)$. All these expressions mean much the same thing as "if A then B." The scientific task becomes to find out how certain it is that when A happens, B happens too? Once that is discovered, it must be determined whether the finding is significant.

Although significance is a human judgment, in scientific terminology, it may simply mean the rejection of the null hypothesis when the results occur by chance 5 percent of the time. "Very significant" in this terminology would mean rejection at the 0.01 level, or 1 percent. The practitioner must decide whether the hazard of rejecting the null hypothesis at any level is too great in comparison with the risk of accepting the substantive hypothesis. Only he can weigh the consequences of the error of accepting an incorrect hypothesis, or of rejecting a correct one.[5]

For example, if the problem is to determine the weight/height ratio of the members of the police department, one might expect a possible impact of the information on a decision concerning the premium rate for group insurance—or whether to offer insurance or not. This is because the weight/height ratio has been found to be rather closely related to longevity.

What is significant here, in the sense of importance, is the actuarial chance of losing a large sum of money from the coffers of the insurance company, if they accept a risk that calls for them to insure the life and health of many whose families collect "benefits" before they have paid about twice as much in premiums. Losses can be averaged out, but in the long run the insurance company tries to figure the full amount of policies paid, plus a sum—often equal in amount—to cover administrative costs. This amount, divided by the number of policies, is the premium for each policy, on the average.[6]

Decisions as to the size of the sample, at what level of significance the sample can be judged to be representative of the entire police department, and whether the longevity of that police department is representative of the longevity of the base-population on which the premium is figured—all these decisions are managerial decisions based not on figures of scientific significance, but rather on figures having to do with the reality of keeping red ink out of the profit-and-loss statement.

Inference About a Future State of Facts

Inference about a future state of facts is based on a present state of facts, *and* on an expectation of the way they will be influenced in the future.[7] Almost all decisions are made on predictions of the future. Although specific techniques or guidelines used for such forecasting are not always apparent, they do exist nevertheless.

One base rule that seems to be used in prediction is the assumption that what is, will be: the future will resemble the present, and experience has proved that this is so. As the future being considered becomes or "approaches" the present as a limit, change will be less likely. It is just as certain, most people think, that the farther the time being considered is from the present, the greater the change we can expect.

Another common guideline to prediction is the presumption that present movements or trends will continue. These patterns of change are various; probably most of them are unknown to us. The trends we do notice, however, we assume will continue. They are identifiable in one scheme as long-term and short-term. Examples are such natural trends and periodicities as the seasons, the tides, phases of the moon, day and night—or, in criminal justice, the rise in crime over years, the regular Christmas rush of holdups and suicides, and the summer rise in assaults.

Despite scientific brave-talk about not being concerned with causation, surely it is appealing to consider the future as bound up in some way with causative forces. When these forces act on variables in understandable ways, the changes in the variables can be predicted. In this regard there is no mathematical substitute for experience and mature judgment.

Neither experience, mature judgment, nor anything else, however, has brought an agreement about the nature and cause of crime. The crime variable escapes predictive or causal understanding, as does most of human social behavior.

Despite this lack of success, if experience and familiarity mean anything, the criminal justice practitioner, in daily contact with problems and issues, should have as much or more wisdom about his affairs than anyone else. He should train himself to consider rational ways to put his potential predictive ability to work by using the predictive methods of science.

Controlled Observation

Some scientists, wary of bias, demand that all observations scored by humans should consist only of the perception that a certain event or behavior has or has not occurred. This would eliminate "guesstimations" of large, medium, or small magnitudes of any observation. To reduce observation to as close a mechanical process as possible would seem to be justified on grounds of error avoidance. On the other hand, much information might be lost if this were the rule. It does appear, however, that for scientific research at least, the more mechanical the data collection procedure, the more the process of inference can be kept to a stage of analysis where it is more rigorously controlled.

That does not increase or decrease the amount of inference, the human activity that cannot be done by machine. Inference occurs in humans constantly as a necessary part of their perception of reality. Descriptive data can come quite close to the fact, but immeasurable amounts of uncontrolled inference will invariably interfere with purely factual findings.

Thus research is plagued and blessed by the same human faculty: inference. Without inference, we know nothing more than what our senses perceive immediately before us without any guide as to what will be the next minute, or even the next second.

Can we surrender individual responsibility and infer that mere collective judgment detects reality? One suspects that there is no absolute way to control observation. We can only try for higher probabilities that we see "the real thing."

Covariance as Inference

The relation between covariance and inference is shown by the scattergram and the regression line superimposed on it (Figure 5-6). In the sample of 196 officers, the taller an officer was, generally the heavier he was too. Thus with the information that a certain unidentified officer in that group is 6 feet tall, it can be inferred that the interval within which his weight *must* fall is from about 167 pounds to about 203 pounds. The inference here amounts to certainty: his weight *is* somewhere between those two figures.

It is possible to be more precise. The cross-tabulations of Figure 5-5 show 19 officers, 72 to 73 inches, about 6 feet tall. Their weights vary from about 160 to about 210 pounds. The precision of the estimate has not increased, but the data do indicate that he is one of nineteen officers, and that he and his fellow 6-footers constitute 9.75 percent of the sample. The chances of selecting a 6-foot-tall officer "at random" from the sample would be about one out of ten.

For even more exact information, one can go to the original data, pick out the nineteen officers and their respective weights, and list them. It would be possible to bet that that subset, or combination, necessarily includes every 6-foot policeman in the sample. There is absolute certainty about that. But the chances of picking one 6-footer from all those choices are only one out of nineteen, or about 5.26 percent.

The regression line crosses the 6-foot interval at 178.9 pounds, but that would be a sure losing bet. Examination of original data shows no 178.9-pound officer. The data does not run to decimal parts. Taking the average of all nineteen officers, 179.7 pounds, does not give a better estimate.

Rounding off to 180 pounds corresponds to the weight of nine officers. Thus if an estimate that the officer's weight is 180 pounds would be exactly correct nine out of nineteen times, or 47 percent, and dead wrong ten out of nineteen times, or 53 percent.

All these inferences appear to be logical, and verifiable. The data confirms the guesses. The general relationships between height and weight can be seen by noting the regression line.

Can such covariance be presumed about the population from which the sample was drawn? As has been stated, if the sample is representative of the population, the scattergram and its regression index may be a good guess as to that unknown, perhaps unavailable, population. The only way to be sure that the sample is representative is actually to measure each element-attribute in the population, and then compare the findings with the sample.

But doing so is often impossible. An alternative is to estimate how frequently the sample is likely to be representative if and only if a truly random sample can be drawn from that population.

Generalizing from Sample of Population

Two Theories. The basic concepts behind the modern practice in generalizing from sample to population is founded on two postulates: a theory of error and the central limit theorem.[8]

According to the theory of error, an error of measurement that is not systematically biased will be equally divided on both sides of an imagined correct value, in a normal distribution. According to the central limit theorem, a series of sample arithmetic means, randomly drawn, will arrange themselves approximately in a normal distribution about the unknown population mean, if the population is large.

It was previously stated that all measurement starts with a standard of comparison. These theories propose such a standard: a "normal distribution" for which there is a specific known formula that can fully describe this curve, and measure the areas beneath it that represent the various frequencies of sets of score-values. Not only does mathematical theory support these two theorems, but also actual observation has tended to show errors distributed in a normal frequency, bell-shaped curve.

With the normal curve as a standard, many previously dark areas of inference can be illuminated. An example is Figure 5-4, where the computer printed out confidence intervals, showing the mean height score as 71.776 inches, with a confidence interval at 95 percent of 71.342 to 72.209. The confidence interval represents a set of possible values that the population-mean may be. It is stated that there is a 95-percent. probability that the confidence interval contains the true value of that parameter.

Generalizing from that sample to the entire population of heights produces a reasonable guess, with a numbered probability of being correctly within a stated range. This is a vast advance over saying, "I guess," or "It is likely." It is justifiably possible to generalize from the sample to the population whether or not the population parameter is actually measured.

It must be remarked that in a given set of samples with numbered confidence intervals, there is no certainty that 95 percent of these intervals will contain the correct value of the parameter of the population. However, in the long run it can be expected, if the samples were chosen at random. Unfortunately, no judgment sample can be defended on rigorously logical grounds.

For example, take the problem of finding the average intelligence quotient of the people residing in Dade County, Florida.

"Judgment" dictates that at least one way to obtain a representative sample would be to provide representation for identifiable groups in the community. Thus of the 1,500,000 or so citizens of Dade County, say 500,000 are of Latin origin, 150,000 of Jewish background, and the rest are Catholics and Protestants. The population, however, is incorrectly partitioned: many of the Latins are also Catholics.

At any rate, the connection between religion and intelligence is doubtful. Partitioning along divisions of residence and choosing the sample by providing representation for each occupational group are both suspect.

As stated before, there is no judgment sample that can be defended on rigorous logical grounds; in fact, most judgment sampling methods are faulty. They offer practicality, but there is always that leap into speculation, that guess about their relevance and validity. There are judgment samples that reach for stratification representation by various levels of income, occupation, interests, professional association, and so on. There are judgment cluster-samples that reach for representation by localities, or other identifiable groups that seem reasonably to demand representation in proportionate amounts in the sample. In every case, however, choice depends on the subjective impressions of the people who do the choosing. All too frequently, this subjectivity calls for a sample of convenient subjects who just happen to be close at hand. Such a sample is cheaper; that often is the main consideration.

If in a given research effort the above-cited sampling methods are in error, it is an error that is easy to understand when one is cognizant of the practical difficulties of drawing a truly random sample. Research must proceed in complete candor, revealing its basic assumptions at all times. If it can offer a numerical statement of probable error, so much the better.

Random Sampling

What has been said so far about confidence intervals and the probability that samples will provide representative indexes is true only if the sample is to be drawn at random.[9] Even when the population is normally distributed, if the sample is not drawn randomly, there is no reason to expect error-filled observations to follow a normal distribution, or to group about a mean. Random sampling demands that each element-attribute that is selected have an equal chance of selection with every other element-attribute.

It is not always easy, in the real world, to arrange circumstances so that each element has an equal probability of being selected out of its population and then placed in the sample. Take what might seem a relatively simple case: choosing a random sample from the officers of a given police department. For each selection to be independent, after each officer is selected, that officer should be returned to the larger group or population so that he has the same chance of being selected again. Each time a researcher happens to choose, say, a 6-foot officer, when drawing an element from the population of such element-attributes, he reduces the number of 6-foot scores still available to choose from. If by chance he happens to draw a good proportion of the available 6-footers in the first few draws, the odds against picking that score will have gone down considerably. To ensure that the individual observations are independent, each and every time a selection is made, there should be an *equal chance* for any of the scores to be selected. If replacement is not made, a corrective factor can be calculated. In a very large population, however, the error is not expected to be substantial, and it is usually ignored if the sample size is less than about 10 percent of the population size.

There is *no* number, proportional or absolute, that would be "the random amount" of 6-footers. Random sampling merely means an equal chance of selection for every possible sample of the same size.

It must be remembered that randomization is a future concept. The term "random sample" is used for simplicity when referring to a sample that has already been drawn by that specific procedure. Once selected, however, that sample is fixed, and there is no more possibility for an equal chance of selection. Cards that have been thoroughly shuffled in what is presumed to be a random manner, and cut so they are ready to be dealt are not in a random sequence any more. They are fixed in value and sequence, and a historical event is not, technically, random.

Nevertheless, the examination of a large number of such samples, selected by the procedures suggested for randomization, has often revealed some stable characteristics. For instance, missiles such as bullets shot from a gun, arrows shot from a bow, or stones thrown at a distant telephone pole will fall in a pattern of deviance on each side of the pole. This target pattern, if the sighting has been true, will generally show most of the hits on or near the pole. Some lesser amount will fall in the immediate vicinity, with a gradual drifting off of shots landing at increasingly greater distances from the target. The accurate marksman will produce a target pattern that centers on the pole and is narrowly distributed on either side.

Consider a marksman, N, whose shots fall into a very narrow pattern centered off to one side. Compare his scores with that of O, whose pattern is open and widely dispersed but centered on the target.

Most range instructors would consider N, with his "small group," to be the better marksman. His sample of shots is more precise, and were he to adjust his sighting to the center of the mark, it is likely that his scores would be consistently higher than O's.

Figure 6-1 is a diagram of this difference in precision and variability, for 1000 shots each. It also compares the results of M, a more average performer.

Note that the area of each of the three curves is the same, and that it measures the 1000 shots fired by each marksman. If only 500 shots were fired by one person, to keep the curves of the histograms in proportion, that curve should have only one-half the area.

Although the curves are different in shape, there is a certain similarity to them: all have a bell-shaped appearance, which is elongated in N's case and

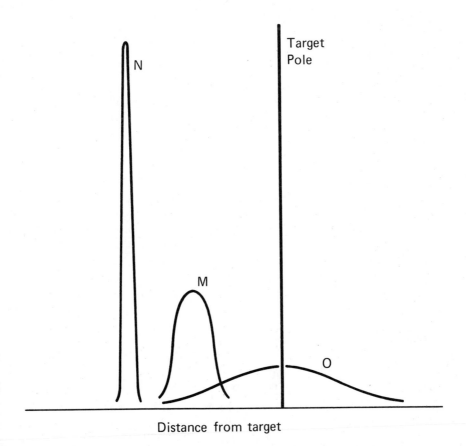

Distance from target

Area under each curve denotes number
of shots fired by each marksman: 1000

Figure 6-1. Normal Curves Showing Differences in Both Precision and Balance-Points (Standard Deviation and Mean).

flattened in O's case. Other similarities are not so visible in this small sketch. In the long run, examination of samples of 1000 shots each will show that an area from a vertical line indicating the mean center of each distribution to where the slope changes from convex to concave would include very close to 34 percent of the shots fired. The same would be true for each of the patterns. Further, twice that horizontal distance would include almost 48 percent of all the shots.

That is a remarkable characteristic that has been noted time and again in different experiences. It can be shown mathematically that in such a situation as this, where scores are made in only two directions—either to left or right of, say, the telephone pole—equally likely errors will balance out about the arithmetic mean as a center point, with expected percentages of the total number of scores at specific relative distances from the center.

These specific relative distances are standard deviations. The standard deviation of a distribution of scores is an "average" deviation from the mean of those scores, and it is calculable in a particular way. (See the glossary.)

The normal curve of distribution of error noted in target shooting is called just that, the normal curve. It has been observed in many other life situations where errors are the result of large numbers of random factors. However, random factors occasionally can cause other curves of distribution to appear.

For example, if in setting down the scores, a consistent unknown factor operates, the curve may be different from the normal one expected. This happens quite frequently, such as when a sample is taken and it is estimated that the mean of the sample is the mean of the population. (This is analogous to taking N's pattern of scores and assuming that the mean of that sample is where the target is). The curve of variation would have a built-in bias that would affect the estimation of the accuracy of other samples or targets.

Doesn't that happen in the real world? Experience as managers and researchers provides information about an observed sample. The best available estimate of the whole population is just that sample. No other information is available, so the sample is used as a basis. Although the manager/researcher may feel that it is not likely to be right for this kind of population estimate, he hopes that it is a reasonable approximation and makes do rather than doing without.

Statisticians have devised the t-distribution curve to help with cases such as this. The areas under this curve are as easily calculated as those under the normal curve. Researchers usually use tables to simplify these calculations when doing them manually. The computer, of course, does them automatically. The studentized mean in Figure 5-4 is from such a t-curve calculation.

Another frequency curve arises in using random expectation as a measuring rule when comparing the variances of two samples—e.g., when one of the samples has been treated, to see if the treatment has "influenced" the sample. Making the smaller variance the denominator and the larger variance the numerator produces a ratio. It is obvious that no ratio can be smaller than one, whereas there is no upper limit on large values. Thus the curve of such ratios will be skewed. Such a curve is called an *F*-curve, and it too has been summarized in tables for manual computation.[10]

Still another way of estimating random expectation as a test statistic is exemplified in cases such as the crossbreaks where a universe of 100,000 was analyzed along the two population variables of sex and friendship (Chapter 2, pp. 14-15).

If one conjectures that these two variables are independent, one could expect each subdivision of each variable to vary in regard to the other as the entire populations differ from each other. In the given example, there are 47,000 men and 53,000 women. If the friendship variable is independent of the sex variable, the proportion of friends among the men should be the same as among the women. That is, out of 100 friends, one should expect 47 men and 53 women.

Since the observed frequencies vary from those expected by chance, is this difference from chance significant? The chi-square distribution is a theoretical probability distribution that can be used to compare observations. It is especially notable because it makes no assumption that the populations involved have a distribution that is normal or otherwise.

Thus *if* one can discover—or guess—what type of distribution chance would provide in a given situation, the observed reality can be compared with the standard provided by the applicable curve of distribution.

How to Use Probability Curves for Comparison

It just happens that measurements made of living things often fall into the normal distribution pattern. This applies to height, weight, and size of various parts of humans and animals, as well as running and jumping, estimating length of lines, colors, and many many other such matters that can be cast into a frequency distribution.

Researchers usually assume that various imagined 'constructs"—such as intelligence, level of knowledge, personal attitudes, and many other human attributes—are distributed normally. The true underlying distribution of these attributes is not known. In fact, we do not even know if reality does contain such attributes. The idea that we call "intelligence," for instance, may not exist in the form of that concept; it may be something entirely different, unimaginable at this time. Certainly there is no universal agreement that what we call intelligence tests, IQs, personality tests, and many other psychometric tests measure these constructs as they are described by the inventors of these instruments.

Whatever these constructs' real equivalents may be, generally when we try to measure them, the observations often assume the normal frequency pattern. But there are exceptions.

If the measure of, say, ability, is too easy for the group tested, the scores will pile up on the side of the distribution that represents success. For example, if policemen were required to push overhead, with one hand, a dumbbell weighing 25 pounds, the frequency distribution would be skewed, or tailed off. The skewing would be in the reverse direction if the task assigned were too difficult for the group, such as the same dumbbell lift attempted by ten-year-old children. The same phenomenon is noticed in written tests. If the examinations are too difficult for the group, the number of high marks tails off, with very few frequencies noted at the high end and most of them bunched at the low side.

The same skewing of distribution is noted when compliance with norms of behavior is tested, e.g., obedience to motor vehicle speed regulations, ingratiating or insulting behavior, and evaluation of other persons. In the last case there is a tendency not to rate anyone below average.

Another group that will give a skewed distribution is one that is composed of two or more distinct populations, such as a group of officers composed of both men and women. Such a group, measured along their population-attribute of height, would tend to fall into a bimodal pattern, centering around a mean height for women, and another distinctly different mean height for men.

In recognition of the fact that the normal distribution does not always represent the true population distribution, which usually remains unknown, other theoretical frequency distributions—such as those discussed on pp. 96-97—are often used to test hypotheses. For further details about theoretical frequency curves, see the glossary at the end of this book, or simple texts on statistics.

The normal distribution is by far the basic pattern in research, and in inference, generally. It was previously mentioned that the sample-mean can be assumed to be the best available estimate of the population-mean. This statement derives from the central limit theorem, which posits that a series of sample-means will approach the form of a normal distribution. This is important because of the way a normal curve rises and falls. It can have an infinite number of specific sizes and shapes as examination of its formula shows (see Table H-1 in the Appendix). It will vary in altitude with the number of scores (generally, varying the scale will change its size); and it will change contour or shape with a change in the dispersion of the scores away from their mean. There are, however, certain characteristics about it that will remain the same, whatever scores or values are involved.

Always about 95 percent of the scores will be within two standard deviations of each side of the mean. Also, about 68 percent will lie within one standard deviation on either side of the mean.

The computer has printed the standard deviation of the scores. Figure 5-4 gives the standard deviation of the height variable in that group as 3.0786. Thus, 68 percent of the scores would be within about 3 inches above and below the mean of 71.8 inches. In round numbers, about 68 percent of the officers in the sample are between 69 inches and 75 inches tall. The confidence limits statistic on the same printout shows that there is a 95-percent probability that this statement will be correct about the entire population within less than one inch. That is scientific inference; it is also quite a great deal to know about a population that has not been measured yet.

That is what the central limit theorem and the preoccupation with normal distribution is all about. Some of the characteristics of the normal distribution are diagrammed in Figure 6-2.

Any score in a sample can be transformed into a z-score (see formula in the glossary), for z-score simply means that the observed score has been measured in standard deviation units. One standard-deviation distance along the horizontal on both sides of the mean takes in about 68 percent of all scores, and two standard deviations on both sides would take in about 95 percent of the scores.

A raw score can be transformed into its z-score equivalent, and it is possible to estimate how many such scores could be expected, in the long run, to be that large or larger.

Thus in a situation where it is reasonable to expect a normal distribution— such as in comparing the means of a long series of samples—if one obtains a

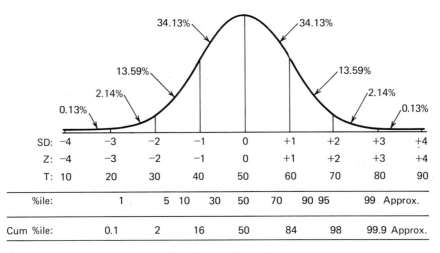

SD:	−4	−3	−2	−1	0	+1	+2	+3	+4
Z:	−4	−3	−2	−1	0	+1	+2	+3	+4
T:	10	20	30	40	50	60	70	80	90

%ile:		1		5 10	30	50	70	90 95		99 Approx.

Cum %ile:		0.1		2	16	50	84		98	99.9 Approx.

SD = Standard Deviation
Z = Z-score (units of SD)
T = T-score (no negative values)
%ile = Percentiles, rounded off
Cum. %ile = Cumulative percentiles, rounded off, in
approximate relative positions.

Figure 6-2. Characteristics of Normal Curves.

sample-mean that scores up around the second standard of deviation (z-score = +2), one can reasonably state that such an occurrence would be expected in only about 5 percent of the samples. Such a result appears not likely to be the result of chance, but rather due to some impelling factor—perhaps the A factor that is being investigated.

To use other theoretical probability curves or distributions, a similar procedure is used. First, the observed raw score-value is transformed into its equivalent theoretical score-value, t, F, or chi-square. Then it is estimated where such a score would come on the frequency curve, and determined whether its likelihood is probable enough to say that chance was, or was not, the probable ruling influence in producing the B consequence of the if-A-then-B relationship that is being investigated.

(Computers can be used to produce the transformed scores, together with the related probabilities involved. Manual computations can be performed in full, or a set of tables can be used.)

Once one appreciates the idea behind this comparison of observations with chance expectations, with practice the procedure soon becomes mechanical. (See Table H-1 for tables of z-scores with their corresponding areas of the normal curve.)

Warning: All the above theoretical curves except the chi-square assume that the distribution of the attribute in the population is normal. Further, all except the chi-square assume equal and continuous levels of measurements; therefore the chi-square test is among those called nonparametric. In recent years there has been an increasing objection to the use of analyses that assume that underlying attributes are normally distributed, and even more objection to assumptions that the scales used are equal-interval scales. Thus there has been an increase in the use of nonparametric procedures, such as chi-square and rank-order measures that do not make such assumptions.

To present a balanced view of this controversy: opposing statisticians think that often the error involved in judiciously making such assumptions is probably small, and that the advantage of the more powerful, searching parametric statistics more than overcomes it. Again, an example of the discretionary aspects of statistics.

Decision-Making Under Risk

In a sense, all managerial decisions are under risk in that they are made in contemplation of a future state of facts that is not certain to happen.[11] If things do not turn out as expected, the decision will be wrong, but if they turn out within reasonable limits of what is expected, the decision may be correct. In addition, not all presently existing facts may be within the decision-maker's knowledge.[12] Despite all these caveats, decisions must be made.

If it is assumed that presently existing facts have been correctly estimated, the success of a decision will rest on correct judgment of the relation of factors beyond the present inspection.

A similar situation exists in Figure 5-6, the scattergram, where the regression line is extrapolated. Extrapolation, the estimation of a quantity that depends on variables by extending the variables beyond their established ranges, is another intuitively acceptable approach to inference. For instance, corresponding weights generally increase with height. Although in the example, where the minimum height is 68 inches and the maximum is 83 inches, it is true that a maximum weight of 241 pounds does not correspond with the maximum height, the general trend is that taller "goes with" heavier. It seems natural to infer that a taller officer would probably be heavier.

The reverse inference seems equally likely: that a shorter officer would weigh less. But there is a limit to this possibility in this population, because officers shorter than 68 inches do not exist in this department. Scientifically stated, the population attribute of height does not include any element of that magnitude.

Perhaps the easiest way to visualize extrapolation is to extend the regression line on the scattergram in either direction. Doing so, however, is not defensible on mathematical grounds, unless there is some knowledge—at least in terms of probability—of the rest of the population.

There are a number of procedures for estimating extrapolation, involving more weight being given to the nearest values, and less weight to those farther. Many practitioners, however, "eye in" such values and thus retain an intuitive feeling for the risk of error.

*Inter*polation, on the other hand, is usually more soundly based in logic and practice. Usually one can take the least sum of the means of known values or proportions thereof, which may be satisfactory when the curve of variation is a straight line. A different procedure would be advisable, however, when the variation is sharply curvilinear. Again, many workers in the field use an eyeing-in method, although if the equation of the curve is known or can be calculated, a more exact method is available.

The problem of decision-making is not merely deciding whether the decision is correct, or even what the probability is that it will be correct. The benefits and costs involved must be considered also.

As little as a 25-percent chance of obtaining a solution to a baffling crime or a crunching traffic situation may be worth a considerable investment of time and money. On the other hand, a 98-percent or almost certain chance of arresting a minor policy pickup man or issuing a traffic citation might hardly be worth the cost of an officer's salary to send him on this errand.

These matters can sometimes be concretized with specific value amounts—in dollars, hours, or other presumed units of costs and benefits. In that case the numerical probability is multiplied by the numerical benefit (or cost, as a minus value). This mathematical expectation could be compared with the equivalent figure of an alternative decision.

For example, say a city has had burglary losses amounting to claims averaging about $5000 per week, in a wave of burglaries for the past two months. The police department had an antiburglary patrol in operation three years previously, initiated by another wave of such crimes. Eventually, this special program of patrol had been abandoned because the incidence of residence burglaries had declined and there were objections to the cost of continuing the unneeded program once the burglary rate had subsided.

Officers experienced with the results of that last operation estimate that burglaries were reduced 50 percent at that time. Today's cost of a similar antiburglary program of public information and patrol is estimated to cost about $1000 per week in equipment and personnel diverted from other duties. The net mathematical expectation of the new operation is clearly a saving of $1500 (50 percent of $5000 minus $1000).

There are, of course, other considerations that are not so easily quantified. One is that the $1000 would come out of the police department budget, leaving that much less for other services, whereas a substantial part of the $5000 in claimed losses are being paid by insurance companies based out of the city.

Can the police manager obtain a supplementary budget allocation? Would the city officials refuse, believing that the benefit of the program would go only to the citizens who were burglarized? The possibility of attracting additional burglars who would consider the city an "easy touch," on the other hand, would be a question of interest to the general community. There would be the possibility of rising rates for burglary insurance. Still another element would be the public's dissatisfaction with the police department for failing to quell the burglary rate with existing facilities. Certainly all these matters are important, though difficult to measure. The effort to measure them, however, would be reasonably within the ability of knowledgeable command personnel, and there would be much benefit from this attempt at rationalizing the decision process.

Some of the items mentioned above touch on an interesting aspect of decision-making that has been called "game theory."[13] The situation where the involved parties stand to gain or lose only to each other is called a zero-sum game. There are certain stakes to be lost or won from the other party. The example of the burglarized city can be viewed either as a zero-sum game, or as a non-zero-sum game, depending on the parties included in the analysis. Managers can consult experts in this type of analysis, but even the nonspecialist's decisions can be based on a clearer view of the alternatives if an attempt is made to use this type of analysis, placing the alternatives in a crossbreak or other tabular form.

One class of decision-making that is specifically the reseacher's problem is deciding whether to accept or reject a supposed relationship—that is, whether to accept or reject a hypothesis.

Hypothesis-Testing: H_1 and H_0

Inferential analysis, faced with complex situations and huge quantities of massed numbers, was forced to develop new techniques, called inferential statistics. The prime objective of formal inferential statistics is to test statements related to hypotheses. The steps taken in hypothesis-testing are as follows:

1. A "substantive" hypothesis is a speculative statement of the relation between two or more variables in short form. The general model is "if A then B." A and B are carefully, and clearly identified, in writing.

2. To test this speculative statement, it must be put into operational terms. One way to do so is by means of a "statistical" hypothesis—the substantive hypothesis is put into statistical terms, stating statistical relations deduced from the relations of the substantive hypothesis. Simply put, measurement units are assigned as required. This statistical hypothesis is often symbolized by H_1. One substantive hypothesis may give rise to many alternative statistical hypotheses, which are usually symbolized by H_2, H_3, H_4, and so on.

    It is important to remember that as the substantive hypothesis reaches for statistical expression as H_1, it moves away from the reality of the criminal justice practitioner. A statistical hypothesis is a prediction, not of reality, but of how the statistics (the measures) will turn out.

3. There is set up against H_1 a denial of that relationship, called the "null hypothesis," symbolized by H_0. H_0 states that the B statistic appears, if it does, only by chance as the random result of a chaotic world. That is if A then B, but only by chance.

4. Attention thereafter is restricted to H_0. The sole object of the research from this point on is to decide whether to accept or reject H_0.

    Acceptance of H_0.

    a. If B can be shown to appear within the limits expected by chance, even when A is present, then it is judged that chance is the controlling influence. In that case H_0 is accepted.

    Rejection of H_0:

    b. If B, however, can be shown to appear either more or less frequently than chance would lead one to expect, it is reasonable to conclude that there is an "inducing factor" that affects the chances of B's appearance.

How much deviance from chance should be sufficient to conclude that the inducing factor is important? It depends on the situation. In research, generally, if in 100 instances where A was applied, B appeared 95 times or more and did not appear only 5 times or less, the result is considered statistically "significant." Such a level of significance of .05 often is calculated by a packaged computer program, as in the examples in this book. A 5-percent "error" in expectation of the repetition of events is acceptable in most behavioral science situations.

That is not the case in many other situations, however. A .05 error is not tolerable in the firing of spark plugs in a gasoline motor, nor in any complicated engine, nor in most mechanical daily affairs about house, kitchen or garage. But in interrogation techniques, in police programs, in large-scale personnel problems, or in most human behavioral issues, for that matter, a .05 error, or level of significance, is acceptable.

The decision is arbitrary, of course, and depends solely on the researcher's judgment. Early in the research, then, before data collection commences, the researcher must decide on a level of significance. This is the point at which he will be satisfied that chance factors have been overcome by A's influence as far as the instant research is concerned.

In testing hypotheses, it is H_0, the null hypothesis, that is tested for acceptance or rejection at a given level of significance. H_1, the statistical hypothesis, is not tested. No matter how many times B appears after A, one cannot infer that the if-A-then-B statement is true or false. Any number of factors other than, or in addition to, A could have induced B to occur.

The general rule, then, is not to test hypotheses directly. The problem is approached by posing the possibility that the conjectured relationship occurred only by chance. Disproving that postulate, by implication one may assume that since chance is not likely to have been the inducing factor, some other factor is involved. Since the only other factor that is certain to be present is A (because it was applied as a treatment), H_1 is tentatively "accepted" under suspect circumstances, solely because H_0 has been rejected.

Thus the acceptance of H_0 results in an unqualified rejection of H_1. But the rejection of H_0 results in only the tentative acceptance of H_1. Simply, we do not seek truth—we merely try to avoid detectable error.

An early example in this book was the universe of people who "possessed" a number of populations of attributes. The population "friendship" was partitioned into a set of two values: friends and nonfriends. These two values were mutually exclusive as defined, and they exhausted the population.

The same thing has been done with the universe-set of one, a particular null hypothesis. The population (P_1) "decisions" was arbitrarily partitioned into "reject" and "accept."

The same is done with the population (P_2) of the attribute that can be called "H_0's agreement with reality," partitioning it into "yes, it does agree," and "no, it does not." The crossbreak is shown in Figure 6-3, which displays all possibilities in an analysis of two dimensions, of two values each. Hence it is a 2 × 2 crossbreak.

It is evident that there are only two possible types of errors: the error of rejecting H_0 when it agrees with reality (Type I error), and the error of accepting H_0 when it does not agree with reality (Type II error).

"Correct" has to do with the correctness of the decision and has nothing to do with "true." "Correct" means merely that B did not occur frequently enough

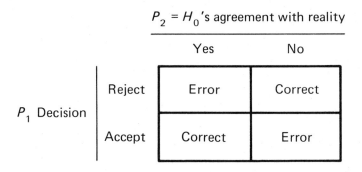

Figure 6-3. Testing a Hypothesis.

to be important. That is, for the particular fact-situation of interest, the if-*A*-then-*B* relationship does not exist to a degree that is useful.

As the crossbreak reveals, it would be an error to reject H_0 when it agrees with reality. The only other possible error (granted no flaw in assumptions or arbitrary judgments) would be to decide to accept H_0 when it does not agree with reality.

Thus all the possible decision-alternatives can be partitioned into "accept H_0" (chance ruled; not if-*A*-then-*B*) or "reject H_0" (chance did not rule; perhaps if-*A*-then-*B* is in reality).

A researcher never accepts a substantive hypothesis in the sense that he believes it to be "true." He accepts it only in the sense that he has rejected chance (H_0).

If he is overeager to find the if-*A*-then-*B* relationship he hopes for, he will tend to reject H_0. If he is pessimistic or overcautious or doubtful about the existence of the relationship, he will tend to accept H_0. The fair cutoff point of how much of a chance the researcher is willing to take can be translated into numbers; it is called a "level of significance."

The level of significance is the probability of making a Type I error. Thus the higher the level of significance—e.g., a change from .05 to .10—the greater the chance of a Type I error. The Type I error, mistakenly rejecting H_0, is a judgment that chance did *not* rule. The researcher may say, "Since I have concluded that chance did not rule, I tentatively accept H_1, my original hope that *A* influences *B*." In effect, he is acting more optimistic about his hope that the relationship exists, and he has implemented his optimism by making it more likely that the decision will go his way.

If, on the other hand, he had set the level of significance to a lower level, such as .001, he would have reduced the chance of a Type I error. Of course, however, he would have increased the chance for a Type II error—that is, his doubt about the relationship would be showing.

The more one tries to avoid a Type I error, the more likely one is to fall into a Type II error. The conservative view is that it is more productive, and less embarrassing, to be doubtful of alleged discoveries than it is to dash about shouting "Eureka, I've found it!" only to be rebutted by later researchers who prove otherwise.

Each researcher, practitioner, or other professional decides whether to be optimistic or skeptical in each situation. A way to quantify this judgment is to choose an appropriate level of significance.

To summarize, here is how an inferential analyst would work out the entire process.

The first arbitrary judgment is to guess at reality: What is the curve of distribution of attribute B in the real entire population, before the interjection of A? If the analyst decides that distribution is probably normal, the curve of Figure 6-2 will apply. (Of course, if he decides the population is of a different curve of distribution of B, he would use that other one.)

The analyst must consider that he is planning to apply the treatment variable, A, hoping it will change the incidence of B an amount he considers significant enough to be useful. Thus he comes to the second arbitrary judgment, a guess at the level of significance that would be appropriate. A common choice is .05. This decision says that if his attribute or relationship (if A then B) occurs in only 5 percent or less of all such events in the entire population, his judgment is that it is too insignificant to be considered a real influence.

In Figure 6-2, the small area to the left of the fifth percentile represents the number of cases expected, in relation to the total population of such cases. If the random sample of observations, as one case, falls into that small area, it could be that it is a rare but possible sample from a normal population—but the chances are against it. The analyst would expect the sample to fall into the much larger area to the right in 95 out of 100 such samplings. Thus the odds favor the sample's being representative of the population as it really exists, and the population we conclude does not exhibit much of an if A-then-B relationship. Of course, if the analyst expected the distribution of values in the population to follow a curve other than the normal one, he would use that other expected probability curve.

Putting it all together: It is important for the criminal justice professional to remember that scientific inference is a matter of reaching for conclusions of varying degrees of probability. These conclusions are human judgments, not observations or empirical findings. They are decisions, not discoveries.

Thus one must pause to consider the question, "What can be inferred when treatment A is applied and B appears a great preponderance of times more than chance would predict? Common experience leans toward expecting the paired observations to continue, knowing the risk that they may not. The procedure of hypothesis-testing merely tries to quantify this. A summary of the process of hypothesis-testing is diagrammed in flowchart form in Figure 6-4.

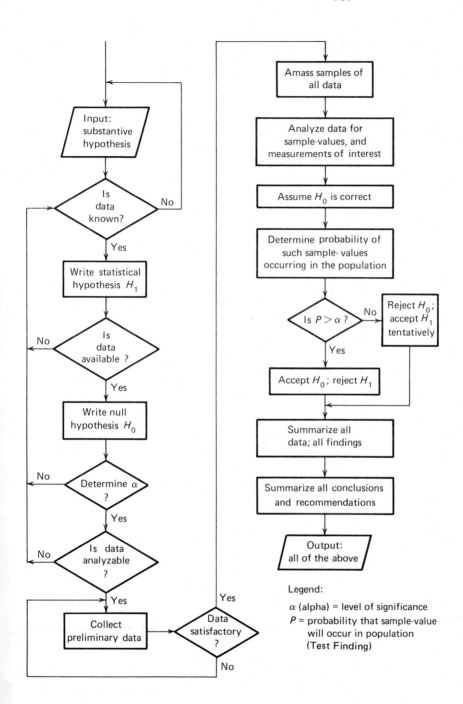

Figure 6-4. Flowchart Illustrating Process of Hypothesis-Testing.

After a researcher chooses a level of significance he seeks a test-finding of the empirical probability, *a posteriori*, that consequence B ensues on the application of treatment A, that is B/A. Usually this test-finding is a sample value.

The level of significance is compared with the test-finding. If the level of significance is *more* than the test-finding, the null hypothesis, H_0, will be rejected, the statistical hypothesis, H_1, will be tentatively accepted and so will the substantive hypothesis.

Some typical situations are in Table 6-1.

Table 6-1
Typical Applications of Level of Significance

α L/S	Test Finding	H_0	H_1	Substantive Hypothesis
.01	.005	Reject	Accept	Accept
	.01	Reject	Accept	Accept
	.02	Accept	Reject	Reject
	.05	Accept	Reject	Reject
	.08	Accept	Reject	Reject
	.10	Accept	Reject	Reject
.05	.01	Reject	Accept	Accept
	.04	Reject	Accept	Accept
	.05	Reject	Accept	Accept
	.06	Accept	Reject	Reject
	.08	Accept	Reject	Reject
	.10	Accept	Reject	Reject
.10	.05	Reject	Accept	Accept
	.08	Reject	Accept	Accept
	.10	Reject	Accept	Accept
	.11	Accept	Reject	Reject
	.13	Accept	Reject	Reject
	.15	Accept	Reject	Reject

7

Computer Printouts

Things Computers Can Do

Computers can receive input of data and specific instructions as to what to do with the data. These instructions are in codes. There are various such codes, called "computer languages."[1]

Large packages of instructions can be stored in a computer's memory, ready to perform whole sequences of operations on data, on call. The call-signals to set these operations off are easily learned from books which list the specific rules to put together the various call-signals of these "packaged programs."

When the proper call-signals are input to a computer that has stored a packaged program[2] it can print-out information, graphics, analyses, and indexes pertaining to given data.

To program a computer, in the first instance, to accept such packaged inputs, requires highly specialized training, not only in computer science, but also in mathematics and statistics. Such a task is beyond the ordinary profession-al, even beyond the research scientist. As mentioned previously, because we are in an age of specialization, the generalist today is not an expert everything, but the professional who oversees.

As a generalist, then, to understand and control research in his agency, he must have a grasp of the meaning and limitations of the indexes that are used in research reports and that are available, even to him, from a computer, should he care to extract them.

Being able to obtain a printout of indexes will not be of much use, however, unless the reader understands their meaning and use. The intelligent utilization of indexes for inference to the fullest requires an understanding of the basic assumptions of the indexes. The ease with which indexes can be obtained in a computer printout has tended to cause improper use and overuse. In spite of this—or because of it—if the practitioner is to grasp the thrust of research reports, he must have some familiarity with the current use of indexes.

All the indexes and measures on Figure 5-4 are listed in the glossary, with applicable formulas. A few additional comments here might be useful.

1. NO. OF OBSERVATIONS is the number of scores whose images have been read from data cards.
2. ARITHMETIC MEAN is what is commonly called the "average." Often called merely the "mean," it is the most useful single index of central tendency available. It is calculated by summing the values of the scores and dividing by the number of scores.
3. STANDARD ERROR OF MEAN is the standard deviation of a sampling distribution of the means, were an infinite number of samples to be drawn. The means of different samples will generally cluster closer together than the original population, or even a single sample. This can be seen in the printout provided where the standard error of mean is smaller than the standard deviation of this sample. The larger the size of the samples, the more closely will their means cluster together.
4. STUDENTIZED MEAN is the mean divided by the standard error of the mean.
5. UNBIASED VARIANCE is the sum of the squared deviations from the mean divided by $N - 1$, and in the long run it equals the variance of the population.
6. STANDARD DEVIATION is the square root of the unbiased variance. It is expressed in the same units as the mean and therefore has an intuitive meaning to the user. In this case the value of about 3 inches standard deviation from the mean of 71.8 inches (rounded off) has real, direct meaning to the non-statistical-minded.
7. COEFFICIENT OF VARIATION is the standard deviation divided by the arithmetic mean. It is usually of interest only when the scores are all of the same sign, as in this example. It indicates the variability of the data values relative to the arithmetic mean.
8. MEAN ABSOLUTE DEVIATION is the average of the absolute deviations of each score from the mean. It has little use, even to statisticians, and serves on this printout as "filler" more than anything else.
9. MINIMUM VALUE is the score lowest in magnitude that has been read by the computer from the data provided.
10. MAXIMUM VALUE is the score highest in magnitude.
11. RANGE is the maximum minus the minimum score.
12. COEFFICIENT OF SKEWNESS is a measure of elongation of the distribution to the right if it is positive; to the left if it is negative. The normal distribution has a coefficient of skewness of zero in this printout. Here there is a distribution that is elongated to the right.

13. COEFFICIENT OF KURTOSIS: in this printout, a normal distribution would have a value of three. The possible values range from zero to a very large figure that would indicate a flattened distribution. Here there is a distribution that is slightly peaked in comparison with the normal curve.
14- RUNS are self-explanatory. They are analyses used to compare the sequence
24. of data values with random data "runs" figures. The object is to aid the researcher in judging whether the data is read in random sequence.
25. CONFIDENCE INTERVAL FOR MEAN AT 95% LEVEL is the interval calculated under the assumption of a normal distribution for the mean of the observations. The probability is 95 percent that the interval contains the unknown population mean. The assumption of normality is *not* restrictive.
26. CONFIDENCE INTERVAL FOR VARIANCE AT 95% LEVEL: There is a 95 percent probability that the interval holds the unknown population variance. Should observations not be at least approximately normally distributed, this interval may be in error, i.e., the assumption of normality *is* restrictive.
27. PERCENTILES are score-values at given percentage totals of scores. Tri-mean is the sum of the twenty-fifth, seventy-fifth, and twice the fiftieth percentile, all divided by four. Percentiles indicate central tendency, but they are not biased by extreme values as is the mean. The fiftieth percentile is the median.

The only descriptive index in common use that is omitted from the list is the mode. The mode is the most frequent score in a data list, and it is easily picked out from the histogram. Should there be two or more clearly identifiable modes of approximately the same frequency, one would be justified in inferring the possibility that the sample contains two quite differentiable groups witin it—e.g., men's and women's heights or weights or physical strength—as measured attribute-populations. So too, if there were a sharp cleavage in age groups in the sample of officers, one might expect the histogram of weight frequencies to show such a bimodality.

Other printouts can be useful for drawing inferences. The most commonly encountered in the literature are cross-tabulation and indexes such as Figure 5-5. The cross-tabulation reports the data in "contingency table form"—that is, a two-way table of discrete categories, or two categories that have been made discrete. Generally the *A*, or independent, variable is marked at the left, vertically, along the rows, different from graphs, which usually show the *A* variable along the horizontal axis. To summarize the remainder of the printout:

Chi-square is a test of independence of the principle of classification used in the cross-tabulation. The cross-tabulation reports the data in contingency table form. It is classified on the principle of "treatment" along the height axis, and "response" along the weight axis. In terms used previously, it tests—in this tabulation only—the hypothesis that height and weight vary independently of each other. Generally it tests hypotheses about frequencies.

This statistic depends on the differences between observed frequencies, and the corresponding frequency of the chi-square curve. If the two sets of frequencies are identical, the value of chi-square will be zero.

The probability distribution of chi-square can be computed and tabulated to give levels of significance. This, however, has been done by the computer. "PROB (CHI-SQUARE .GT. 402.04) = .0000" is a statement that the probability that chi-square will be greater than the given figure of 402.04 is less than .0001, which is the level of significance. This indicates a very high probability that height and weight in fact do have a relationship, but there is no comment on the strength of the relationship.

However, in the example, the cell counts of the cross-tabulation include many that are less than five values. This technically weakens chi-square. Of course, the number of scale divisions for the cross-tabulation could be reduced, which would increase the cell count in each cell so as to validate the chi-square figure, but that would lose much information that should be retained. In any case the scattergram showed the same relationship visually, in a more direct fashion. Of course, if there are many "strikeovers," it would be difficult to read the scattergram. But that same deficiency in the data that vitiates the information value of the scattergram would increase the cell count in the cross-tabulation and increase the validity of the chi-square.

Normalized chi-square is a transformation of the chi-square into standard deviations from the chi-square curve, which at 132 degrees of difference is almost the same as the normal curve.

The remaining indexes on Figure 5-5 are measures of association and, in a sense, correlation coefficients too. This is because they summarize the strength of the bivariate relationship. They supplement cross-tabulations based on nominal and ordinal level variables, with only a few categories.

Any index designed for nominal or ordinal level measurement can be used for higher-level interval or ratio measures because the higher scales include the lower scales. The reverse is not true: an index able to use information contained in the higher (interval and ratio) scales cannot find this information in the lower levels.

The remaining indexes are encountered only rarely in research reports:

Phi is a measure of the strength of relationship for a 2 × 2 table. It is zero when no relationship exists, and +1 when the relationship is perfect either on the main or minor diagonal. Since the example is not a 2 × 2 table, phi is not applicable.

The *contingency coefficient* is another measure of association, but it can be used for a table of any size. The no-relationship situation is shown by zero, but the maximum relationship will depend on the size of the table. Therefore it can be used only to compare "square tables," which have the same number of rows and columns.

Cramer's V is used for large tables. A large value signifies strong relationship; zero indicates no relationship.

Kendall's S is the number of concordant pairs minus the discordant pairs (see DCR and DRC below).

Standardized S is Kendall's S transformed to a standard score so that different-sized samples can be compared. Kendall's coefficients of correlation can be either positive or negative.

Tau-C is for nonsquare tables of two ordinal variables. It is one of the series of Kendall correlation coefficients.

DCR and *DRC* are the Somer's coefficients of correlation, derived from Kendall's S, but adjusted for rows and columns.

Any judgment of the value of complex statistical analyses using the more infrequently used indexes must depend on particular circumstances.[3] The guidelines for criminal justice professionals can be simply stated: (1) use the best advice available, and (2) remember that generalizations are no better than the samples providing the data.

There are two remaining statistics, Spearman's rho and Pearson's *r*, that are not on the printout but will be encountered more frequently than the last few.[4]

Spearman's rho, like tau-C, is a nonparametric correlation, with no assumption about the distribution of cases. It appears in reports now more frequently than ever. Both rho and tau are designed for merely ordinal level data. They can handle a large number of such ranks on each variable. Basically, both are designed to aid in deciding where two rankings of the same cases are similar.

Pearson's product-moment correlation, *r*, is very often used in reports, correlating interval and ratio-level variables with many categories. Frequently a scattergram will be presented in the same report to give a picture of the data.

Both Spearman's rho and Pearson's *r* vary from zero for no relationship to +1 for a perfect, direct relationship along the major axis, and a −1 for a perfect inverse relationship along the minor axis. (As mentioned before, in STATJOB printouts, such as Figure 5-4, the major axis moves *down* as the *x* values increase to show a direct relationship.)

This is in contrast to a handmade draftsman's scattergram, where a direct relationship would show the axis moving up from left to right. That is merely convention. In this particular packaged-program, the computer reverses the plot to save computer time and storage space.

Considerable inference can commence with a study of indexes. Although one can be more probably correct inferring only within a sample, rather than leaping to generalizations about a population of attributes that have not been measured, still the great value of such generalizations tempt both the daring and the unsuspecting. Nevertheless, when conditions are favorable—namely, when not only is the existence of the presumed relationship highly probable, but it additionally exhibits great strength—most researchers and also most professionals would be willing to hazard an inference. Further, most would be willing to speculate hopefully on extending the presumption of pattern to values beyond the scale of the sample.

One of the main differences between the computer and the human is that if you feed guesswork into a computer, you get guesswork back. The machine has no intuition, no insight, no inspiration. Most importantly, the machine has no grasp of where it should ultimately go.

No, the computer is densely, exasperatingly literal. One must admit, however, it does have a certain *Karma*, and fascinates those who are once exposed to it.

Appendixes

Appendix A:
The Research Proposal

A research proposal is the strategic plan of a research work project. It may be as simple or as detailed as the writer pleases depending on his purpose. It may be a phrase such as "let's look into this relationship," or it may be a complex proposal for many millions of dollars to fund research for the federal government (see Appendix E).

When the research proposal is completed, ideally it will include all details of the proposed research, possibly even tactical plans for phases requiring special planning (see Chapter 2, pp. 20-29). Ordinarily, the research proposal will contain at least some information about each of the following:

1. *Title* of the proposed study or project, and any other necessary identification data.
2. *Purpose* and objective of the study (see Chapter 3).
3. *Problem area(s)* identified. If an authority has assigned a problem for solution, it usually does so in specific words. If this can be called the "problem as given" (PAG), it should be differentiated from the problem as it is narrowed down to a specific task. This "problem as perceived" (PAP) is the way to make the problem manageable and within one's ability to handle it. E.g., your PAG may be "crime," and your PAP may be "how to increase patrol." Thus you will be interested in:
   a. limiting the problem to the PAP
   b. defining all possibly ambiguous terms
   c. Identifying assumptions and biases
   d. Analyzing to reveal collateral problems
   e. Explaining of the importance of the PAG.
4. *Review of literature* already covered, with indication of the areas that are to be reviewed. It is useful to
   a. cite specifics as to where PAP stands in regard to all that has been thought and done before
   b. reveal prior use of data sources, analytical methods, and the reasons why proposal promises better results than prior efforts.
5. *Hypotheses* (see Chapter 6, pp. 103-109):
   a. presentation of substantive hypotheses in the simplest possible form, as a tentative solution to PAP
   b. operationalized form of substantive hypotheses, in measurable form if at all possible (H_1, H_2, etc.)
   c. null form of hypotheses (H_0), if applicable
   d. Specification of levels of measurement
   e. Specification of the chosen level of significance
   f. Justification of all of the above.

117

6. *Research design:*
   a. identification of all variables: independent and dependent, and extraneous variables anticipated; explanation of all instrumentation
   b. Identification of samples and populations
   c. Specification of the exact data to be sought, and why, when, where, and how it will be collected, together with the persons and places involved in data collections
   d. Specification of control groups, and control procedures; criteria for admission of data; guards against contamination of data
   e. Description of all analytical methods planned and why they are appropriate.
   f. Justification of all of the above, in the particular mix chosen.
7. *Special qualifications* of the researcher and staff should be listed, as part of the arsenal of resources available.
8. *Evaluation and monitoring:* Explanation of all such procedures planned for this project.
9. *Time-table and budget:* These two items should be coordinated so as to indicate the time each sum (and other resource) should be available and expendable. All necessary procedural details and information should be tied in here, e.g., persons' addresses and phone numbers, offices to be contacted, and so on.

The preceding list is merely a set of guidelines for the plan of the project. It would not be reasonable to spend much time or effort on a plan for a small research project.

Circumstances alter cases. Often the major purpose of the research proposal is to persuade. An example of this would be applications for government funds for research (see Appendix E), which while fulfilling the function of a strategic plan, contain even detailed tactical plans for the proposed research, and are fundamentally designed to convince the funding authorities of the worthy potential of the research and to formally submit to budgetary allocations and evaluative conditions.

If a large number of assistants will be involved in the proposed research, the proposal may detail their specific duties. Collection procedures could be explained; annexed copies of schedules, survey questionnaires, and report forms are appropriate.

For control purposes, it may even be useful to list particular times and dates for assistants to collect data.

Each scientific research proposal will be different, just as all strategic plans differ. Free flows of imagination, brainstorming, "idea meetings," canvasses of interested and qualified people—all can be very productive in developing good proposals. A strong effort here will perhaps be more fruitful than at any subsequent time, for this document sets the direction and outlines the pattern of all the labor to follow. Also, if it is sufficiently detailed, it will be referred to again and again, until the last step is taken, the final report prepared, and the last evaluative review completed.

Appendix B:
One Way to Organize
a Research Project

Research projects have been as varied as the people who have undertaken them. This appendix lists a set of guidelines for organizing a fairly large project. If any item clearly does not apply to a specific research, determine what other means will perform the function of the procedure deleted.

1. *Diary:* Maintain a diary of *all* action and thought regarding the project, even the most minute. This document often becomes the most valuable single work of the effort.
2. *Research proposal:* Prepare a detailed research proposal, detailing all planned work (see Appendix A).
3. *Proceeding:* Perform all the tasks outlined in the proposal, according to the time schedule, except as revised.
4. *Reviewing:* All actions should be constantly reviewed from this point on. Constantly compare plans with performance in the diary.
5. *Monitoring:* Monitoring is the ongoing oversight of all activities to provide immediate corrective feedback. It is as much attitude as process, and should be considered when setting up each activity to provide for immediate corrective action in the event of error.
6. *Data analysis:* Use expert help to analyze data according to methods previously set forth in the research proposal. Doing so will involve constructing models, graphic presentation, tabulations, mathematical manipulations, or whatever experience, logic, or expert advice recommends.
7. *Findings:* Summarize the data in "findings." Do the findings appear to be well substantiated by the data items? Have you overlooked relevant data? Are the summary indexes appropriate? Are there any unstated assumptions in any part of your methodology, including the analytical methods? Have you included *all* information required by another researcher for replication? Would you expect another researcher to arrive at different findings? Why?
8. *Conclusions and recommendations:* Present conclusions, clearly separating them from findings of fact. Point out, however, the specific findings upon which conclusions and recommendations are based, including the rationale involved.
9. *Research report:* This document is to be prepared *after* all the above work has been completed.
10. *Evaluation:* Obtain the most disinterested and qualified evaluation team possible to inquire into every phase of the finished research and report. Provide them with all information and materials they may require, such as diary, original data, worksheets, subsidiary task reports, etc. Then they should be left alone to complete their job.

11. *Storage:* Store all original data, worksheets, diary, and so forth in a safe place for possible reference during later work in the same subject area. Include, too, the evaluators' reports and your own comments in (dis)agreement. Include all suggestions that might be useful should a similar project be contemplated in the future.

All the above is merely *one* way to organize a research project. If a different way would serve better, by all means that route should be followed. The important thing about problem-solving, scientifically or otherwise, is to get about doing the job and completing it successfully. Success is measured not by procedural regularity but by the solution of the problem.

Appendix C:
How to Write a
Research Report

Content

Just as there is no single correct way to write a research proposal, the field is wide open to creative imagination in report-writing. The report should reflect an intelligent, honest effort to explain all important matters. To be truly scientific in presentation, it should permit the reader to replicate the research effort in every essential respect. If the report does not convey this much information, it can justifiably be denied status as a scientific report. It may, however, be an abstract, a summary, a progress report, or other document making whatever statements or claims the researcher cares to declare.

Because the researcher has just completed the "working" part of his research (see Appendix B), he is the best judge of what must be included to permit replication.

It is a good idea to make a checklist of all points of detail and information that must be included. It is also a good idea to compare the list with other such lists. The list in Appendix D is an example of an absolute minimum. It is important not to leave anything out; even doubtful items should be included. Unless everything is included, not only will the researcher not receive the recognition to which he is entitled, but he may forget the information, too. The masses of data and papers will shortly become incomprehensible; some documents will stray. The final report and evaluation often will be all that is left after a remarkably short time.

Format and Style

Much depends on the researcher's level of mastery of the chosen communication medium. While some research reports have used such media as sound motion pictures, audio tapes, transparencies, and even posters and wall-sized pictures, generally a report will be a typed set of pages.

Good usage is required for such a report. Either the assistance of a qualified writer is necessary, or recourse to dictionaries, grammars, and style and usage manuals. Granted the availability of writing skill, the special style and format of technical and report-writing is outlined in many specialized manuals. Typographical conventions and style manuals have been developed for each of the several disciplines. Criminal justice has not reached this stage yet.

The scientific community generates about 6 million pages of scientific and technical information a year. No researcher can keep up with the literature in his own specialty, let alone reach far across boundaries for refreshing, cross-fertilizing ideas in other disciplines.

There has been a continuing drive to restrict format and style to a standard form to facilitate machine-reading, analysis and abstract writing, and most of all storage and retrieval. Such standards, however, have not yet been widely accepted.

Each professional journal has its own code of rules for punctuation and style, which must be followed if the journal's cooperation is desired. Thus the American Psychological Association has issued a publication manual for use by all report writers in that field. The United States Government Printing Office has issued a *Style Manual.* Many universities use Kate L. Turabian's *A Manual for Writers*[1], which has a helpful section for scientific papers. If the report is aimed for a particular publication, it is best to examine copies of that publication, especially in the criminal justice field. A list of journals in criminal justice is appended to this book. The style of each differs from all the others. Very few of the articles in these journals, however, are truly scientific research reports. Most such reports are too voluminous to be published in full in the space available.

University libraries keep files of dissertation papers, which often are research reports, of their own students. Most libraries also have copies of the *Index of Dissertations*, which will identify and locate literally thousands of dissertations all over the United States. A good library will have bound copies of collected research reports of many of the "hard" sciences, particularly chemistry, which seems to be well circulated. There will be many of the shorter research reports in the various professional journals of each discipline, but one must be selective in choosing among them for the best models.

Many of the lengthy reports are bound as books and catalogued in the library as ordinary books and so placed on their shelves. Often they are in the *Index of Dissertations* and can be located by title and author.

Evaluation

While not every scientific paper will have an evaluation section included, it is becoming more and more customary to do so. In any case, even if not included in the report itself, a separate well-documented evaluation should be prepared.

There has been much disappointment with all of criminal justice research for inadequate, often self-serving claims that have been formulated and proffered as evaluations of the various programs and experiments funded by the federal government. Actually, there should be a continuous process of evaluative feedback, or monitoring, all during the course of the research project (see Appendix B).

The final evaluation, at the end of the project, should be a complete reappraisal of all aspects of the work performed by as unbiased a process as can be devised. If the effort is large enough, it may be advisable to hire an outside evaluator or even a team of evaluators.

The evaluation is itself a research project, and when the size of the subject warrants, it should be conducted with all the formal procedures and safeguards of the prime research. This would include an "evaluation proposal" as a strategic plan, tactical plans, diaries, and control measures.

Especially when large sums have been expended, it becomes mandatory to have the most careful and intensive evaluation practicable. The thrust of the evaluation is not only to document all the activity and changes in the dependent and independent variables, but also to show what changes, if any, resulted from the influence of the independent variables and not from other factors.

Only by such careful evaluation can the full benefits of research be obtained, and wasteful repetitive duplication avoided. On the bottom line, the point of a program is whether it produced a specific result. In our lifetime we may never know ultimate truth of this matter, but careful evaluation can help obtain the most for the least.

Among the questions pondered by the evaluator is whether the researcher did not ask the correct questions because he had too great a stake in the answers. It would not be amiss for the evaluator to ask the same question of himself as he prepares his evaluation, for his evaluation will be considered by others, and itself evaluated. An evaluation report read without the research report it concerns, and without whatever response the research people provide, may easily tend toward a very biased view.

Therefore the research report, in final form, should seek to contain evaluative comment with appropriate explanatory comment, either in dissent or in confirmation.

Appendix D:
How to Read a
Research Report

There are many ways to read a report, almost as many as there are purposes for the report. The purpose of an alleged research report may not be explicit, or the stated purpose may not be the real one. Part of the reading effort is to determine the writer's purpose so as to evaluate whether he has attained that purpose. Another part of the effort can be to determine whether the report really serves the true function of a scientific report by providing all information necessary to replicate the project, *and* by abiding by the general requirements and approaches of science.

Often a checklist, prepared either in advance or after a quick preliminary reading, is useful in appraisal. One such checklist that has been found useful is printed here. It consists of a series of items, scaled from 1 through 5, for appraisals of each quality described from very bad through bad, average, good, and very good. A score of 5 for each item would be the highest grade on such an evaluation.

1. Organization (title, table of contents)
2. Introduction to problem; implications
3. Review of literature
4. Hypotheses: clear? operationalized?
5. Population and samples: clear and justified?
6. Data collection criteria and instrumentation
7. Data analysis: fully explained?
8. Objective findings: substantiated?
9. Conclusions and recommendations: supported?
10. Bibliography and format

The listed items should be an absolute minimum and should be visible in every report, unless they are not applicable to the specific research involved.

The scoring provides a maximum of 50 and a minimum score of 10. To transform these raw scores to a base zero ranging to 100, subtract 10 from the raw score and multiply by 2.5. The transformed scores will then provide a range from 0 percent to 100 percent as a derived score for various reports that can be evaluated in relation to each other.

The above is not the only way to read, or score, a research report; it is not necessarily even a good way. It is merely a way designed to clarify the absolute minimum detail that would be expected in reports and to give exposure to the use of transformed scores.

The usefulness of this list and scoring system would depend entirely on the particular reports and the purpose of the analysis and scoring.

Appendix E:
How to Apply for
Government Funds
for Research

One of the important tasks of the criminal justice professional is to apply to various government offices for funds to support programs and research projects. Most programs involve research and evaluation to some degree; many consist wholly of research and evaluation.

These applications can be viewed as a variety of a research proposal (see Appendix A), designed to persuade the government to provide money.

The way to attain this purpose is to discover what funds are available, present the proposed research as being eligible for such funding, demonstrate convincingly the value of the research, assure rigor in the research design, and suggest budgetary and evaluative conditions.

Whether the funds are to come from local, state, or federal office, there is not much difference in the procedure. Since government regulations frequently change and forms and offices are phased in or out from time to time, the procedural requirements discussed will be general.

Guidelines

Basically, all these applications require:

1. rigid adherence to all formal requirements set forth in statutes and regulations
2. specific information in lavish detail
3. compliance with all time limitations
4. compliance with evaluation requirements.

Since in most instances the ultimate source of funds is the federal government, the requirements of the Washington offices are the most stringent. They are not unduly so, however, and merely call for precise statements about the contemplated research, and certain additional safeguards that have been found necessary.

Procedures

In a typical situation to make application for the Law Enforcement Assistance Administration funds, the following guidelines are applicable:

1. Telephone, and follow-up with a letter, to local, state and regional federal offices of LEAA requesting all forms and regulations pertaining to the type of project in mind.
2. In the same telephone call and follow-up letter, request copies of all relevant laws and regulations. If that is unavailable, require that office to give the citations to those laws and regulations so that they can be located elsewhere.
3. When the forms and regulations arrive, photocopy them immediately; they will be in constant demand and will require the personal inspection of every person who is to work on them.
4. Carefully examine the laws and regulations for all possible applications to the agency and its objectives. The office, or the particular research, may be entitled to apply for funds from previously unknown agencies, for the most unexpected purposes. Often maintenance, rent, overhead, or other expenses will be fundable by one source, whereas salaries and field expenses will be entitled to aid from another. Thus it may be useful to split requests, applying to two or more sources for one research project. There are persuasive elements in this. Not only is less money needed from each sponsor, but also it conveys to them a comforting feeling, knowing that there is another agency sharing the responsibility and risk.
5. Examine the application forms very carefully. Invariably they are divided into "parts," each part calling for information of a different character. Collect all the information needed for each part, and make draft copy of the entire application document.
6. Go through the draft in minute detail. It is important to make each part consistent with every other part. There should be no mistakes in arithmetic—not even the most minor ones. It should be reasonable and convincing, but not bombastic or overreaching. Nothing should be said in any section of the application that is contradicted by any other section.

A Typical Application Form

As of 1976, the Law Enforcement Assistance Administration application forms for research funds consist of four parts. Each part calls for specific information, and some of the parts are subdivided into several formal categories.

Part I. General Administrative Information. This part is a cover page, which notes that the form calls for "Project Title, Funding Category, Area in Which Application is Made, Anticipated Subgrant Period," and similar matters.

This part requests the names of the people to be most concerned, such as applicant, chief financial officer, implementing agency, and project director. It also calls for an abstract of some 200 words.

Part II. Project Plan and Supporting Data. This section is usually divided into four subsections: statement of the problem, measurable objectives, procedure and timetable, and resources.

The LEAA considers all these topics to be interrelated, so therefore they should be written to reflect that relationship. Need—for the target population—should be clearly defined, with documentation. State manageable objectives, which, if met, will have the planned effect on the problem and on the target population(s). Be realistic in organizing procedures and allocating resources, with an aim to attaining the project objectives.

Part III. Budget Component. A budget summary for the entire grant period is customarily required here. This summary should include all funds—local, state, and LEAA—that are planned to be expended. Also, an estimate of future support that will be required is requested, as well as all prior fundings for this project.

This part also requires a separate schedule of personnel costs, separated as to monthly salaries, fringe benefits, and percent of time to be spent on the project. Professional services other than regular personnel, with cost estimates, should be cited. Contract and consultant service charges should not be omitted. Schedules of travel costs must be prepared, as anticipated, listing purpose, by whom, and itemized costs. An equipment cost schedule is another separate document required, as well as a schedule of construction costs. Finally, two last schedules are required: "other operating expenses" and "indirect costs."

This part closes with a "budget narrative" and a "fiscal questionnaire." The budget narrative calls for a justification and explanation of the items shown on the budget, identifying all data by the major budget categories. The fiscal questionnaire considers such important areas as "hard cash match," special matching fund requirements on personnel compensation, rental of buildings, and so on.

Part IV. Compliance/Administrative Component. In certain cases "Resolutions and Certifications" from the governing board of the grantee are required. These documents are to assure the granting agency that statutory and regulatory conditions are complied with.

Appendix F:
How a Nonexpert Can
Use Computers

It is not necessary to be able to do statistical calculations to extract descriptive statistics that will be useful to the criminal justice practitioner. Actually, not even a knowledge of algebra is necessary, and only the most rudimentary arithmetic is involved.

It is far more important to understand the practical meaning of the simpler indexes. The ability to comprehend what the indexes say about the data is more important than the ability to hand-compute what a computer can do so much better and faster.

Most researchers have found the following simple indexes of most general utility: arithmetic mean, median, mode, range, standard deviation, percentiles, confidence intervals, and significance levels. Each of these is discussed in detail elsewhere in this book (see Chapter 7 and Glossary).

Hand-held computers are capable of taking data input, and at the push of a button outputting arithmetic mean, standard deviation, and other indexes. The greatest flexibility, however, is offered by using published packaged programs.

In either case the first requirement is to examine the data. What are their levels of measurement? How much are there? Can they be graphed? Can they be cross-tabulated? What is the best analysis for these data? If the data are not too numerous, categorical, and do not require advanced analysis, often a simple graphic or cross-tabulation will be all that is required—and if the number of values is not too great, manual treatment may be the best way. If, however, they are numerous, or complex calculations are involved, one might consider using a computer.

Guidelines

The procedure to use a packaged program is as follows:

1. Find out which packaged program(s) the computer center can handle, and choose one.
2. Obtain the book describing how to use that packaged program.
3. Carefully, and literally, follow the directions in the book to prepare the control-program and the data in the form demanded, calling the desired indexes.
4. Input to the computer the control-program and the data by giving them to the person in charge of the computer installation.
5. Receive computer printout of indexes in due time.

Usually the packaged program will require that input be on punched cards. Figure F-1 shows the control deck used to obtain all the computer printouts in this book in a single pass at the computer. The computer reads the cards one at a time, from the front of the deck to the back.

Most of the indexes presented in the figures in this book are inappropriate for the particular data from which they were extracted by the computer, as was explained previously. They are presented merely for demonstration purposes. The control deck for the much fewer indexes that are actually required in a real managerial problem would be much smaller. An examination of the alpha-numeric comment on each of the cards gives an idea of the various "calls" each card makes on the computer, even without the translation given by the book that outlines vocabulary and syntax for this packaged program (STATJOB).

If the computer installation can handle demand, or conversational, another alternative is to input the data in the programming language called for by the keyboard terminal, e.g., BASIC.

Chapter 7 of this book can be used as a checklist of data indexes usually available, with the corresponding explanations of the types of data for which they are adaptable.

If the computer center is programmed for the STATJOB package, and if the same indexes listed in the printouts in this book are wanted:

1. Punch cards as listed in Figure F-1. (This control deck of forty-five cards must be supplemented by cards punched with the data relevant to the inquiry, and inserted after the fifth control card shown in Figure F-1.)
2. Submit the entire deck to the computer center operator for input to the computer.
3. Receive the printout pages, which should be similar to those in this book; since the data will be different, however, the indexes will have different values.

If the computer is not programmed for STATJOB, the operator will know packaged programs to which it is adapted. There is a book that summarizes the syntactical rules for each package. The instructions must be followed precisely; the slightest error, even in one punched card, will probably "bug" the entire operation, and the bug will have to be removed before the deck will run properly.

Various sets of data can be used with the same control deck as long as the data fit within the constraints of the packaged program. But these limits are so broad that they are of no hindrance whatever. Whatever they are, however, the book outlining the packaged program will clearly list them. Thus once the control deck is available, it can be used for any problem of that kind for an indefinite number of "passes," each pass providing all the list of the indexes "called" from the computer as it reads the data.

```
"FIN
BEGINDATA*******INPUT OF OFFICERS
RUNRB MODEL 1   *DEPVAR(2),INDEPVAR(1),COEFCORR
RUNRB I/FORMAT *(F2,1X,F3)
RUNRB INPUT     *NVARS(2),SDFFILE
BEGINPROG*******REGAN2
BEGINDATA*******INPUT OF OFFICERS HEIGHT&WEIGHTS CORRELATION
RUN 5 I/FORMAT  *(F2,1X,F3)
RUN 5 INPUT     *NVARS(2),SDFFILE
BEGINPROG*******DSTAT2
BEGINDATA*******INPUT OF OFFICERS HEIGHT&WEIGHTS SCATTERGRAM
RUNRB DISP1,1   *YVAR(HEIGHT),XVAR(WEIGHT),PLOTPRT,HEIGHT(5),LENGTH(5)
RUNRB VNAMES 1 *V1IS HEIGHT,V2IS WEIGHT
RUNRB I/FORMAT *(F2,1X,F3)
RUNRB INPUT     *NVARS(2),NOBS(1000),SDFFILE
BEGINPROG*******PICT1
BEGINDATA*******INPUT OF OFFICERS HEIGHT&WEIGHTS BIVARIATE ANALYSIS
RUNRB TAB 1     *ROW(1),COL(2),TABLE(FREQ,PPLANE),CHISQ,TAU
RUNRB SCALE 2   *2/LB/140/150/160/170/180/190/200/210/220/230/240/250//OTHER
RUNRB SCALE 1   *1/LB/68/69/70/71/72/73/74/75/76/77/78/79/80//OTHER
RUNRB VNAMES 1 *V1IS HEIGHT,V2IS WEIGHT
RUNRB I/FORMAT *(F2,1X,F3)
RUNRB INPUT     *NVARS(2),SDFFILE
BEGINPROG*******CROSTAB2
BEGINDATA*******INPUT OF OFFICERS HEIGHTS, UNIVARIATE ANALYSIS
RUNRB OUTPUT    *PERCENT,CI(.05),RUNS
RUNRB HIST      *NORMAL(1/13/68,81)
RUNRB VNAMES 1 *V1IS HEIGHT,V2IS WEIGHT
RUNRB I/FORMAT *(F2,1X,F3)
RUNRB INPUT     *NVARS(2),NOBS(196),SDFFILE
BEGINPROG*******UNISTAT1
&STJ
&END
&ADD,D SORTOUT.
&DATA,IL LIST.
&ADD INPUT.
&CS CCOO        1       1       80      1,2/4,3/
&SORT
&END

    Insert Data Deck Here

&DATA,IL INPUT.
&ASG,T INPUT.
&ASG,T SORTOUT.
"EBCDIC
"RUN IISRSC,I0130F,UCS100389221,3,100/1000
```

Figure F-1. Runstream (of Punched Cards).

While learning about computers, however, one should use smaller, hand-held computers as much as possible. Not only are they more generally available to criminal justice professionals, but actually doing the work leads to a better comprehension of the implications of the indexes. There is one disadvantage: all graphics must be prepared manually.

Graphics are best drawn with the guidance of such books as are listed in the selected bibliography, which refer to the multitude of graphs and graphic analyses that can be constructed with only minimal training. There is no space here to explain the simple conventions and techniques that a good draftsman will use. Suffice it to say, however, that the objective of the good graphic is that it be comprehensible to the uninitiated.

A good draftsman, capable of making graphic representations of data, is a precious resource and as specialized in his field as computer programmers, statisticians, or behavioral scientists are in theirs.

Except for advanced statistical analysis—which is beyond this book, and outside the capacity of the average criminal justice professional—the main advantage of the large computer installation is the quick availability of graphics, which can be easily apprehended by justice personnel.

Appendix G:
Glossary

α: Probability of a Type I error, i.e., rejecting the null hypothesis (H_0) when it is correct.

ALGOL: A programming language.

Analysis: The separation of a whole into its parts.

Arithmetic Mean: An index of central tendency of a distribution of scores, often inaccurately shortened to "mean" (q.v.). Calculated as the sum of score-values divided by the total number of scores.

Average Deviation: A measure of the amount, but not the sign, about the arithmetic mean, of the deviations of the scores. Defined as:

$$\frac{\Sigma \mid X_i - \overline{X} \mid}{N}$$

β: Probability of a Type II error, i.e., accepting the null hypotheses (H_0) when it is false.

BASIC: A programming language well adapted to the interactive mode of the computer.

Batch Mode: Input to a computer via prepared batch of data, all presented at the same time with control input. See *Conversational Mode* as an antonym.

Bivariate Analysis: The analysis of two variables as to when or how they relate. "If A then B" is another statement of this functional relationship in a general form. Usually one variable is considered independent, and the other is considered dependent. Often, however, the states of independence or dependence can be reversed in analysis.

BMD: A packaged program facilitating handwritten computer programming.

"Bug": Undiscovered error. Often applied to problems of newly written programs.

Card: In this book, refers to a paper card 7 3/8 in. by 3 1/4 in. with eighty vertical columns for data, in twelve alphanumerical rows; a computer card, used to store and input information to a computer.

Central Tendency: The general thrust of a frequency distribution. A typical value, e.g., arithmetic mean, median, mode, etc.

Chi-Square: A theoretical frequency distribution often used to test hypotheses about proportions and frequency counts. This distribution is not symmetrical; it is skewed to the right, ranging from zero to $+$ infinity. As a sample increases in size, this distribution approaches a normal shape. It is used to compare frequencies obtained (f_o) with frequencies expected (f_e) by this chi-square distribution:

$$\chi^2 = \frac{(f_o - f_e)^2}{f_e} \, .$$

This test is very frequently used to compare values in crossbreaks to determine statistical significance with the help of tabled values.

COBOL: A programming language adapted to business operations because it easily handles large inputs and outputs with small amounts of calculation. Source of the name: COmmon Business Oriented Language.

Code: Any system used to symbolize data.

Coefficients of Correlation: A number of different types of indexes of relation, indicating by value, and often sign, the varying degrees of the relationship were it to be expressed linearly.

Coefficients of Kurtosis: A number of different indexes of "peakedness" of a frequency distribution, compared with a normal curve as a standard. This is a measure of the concentration of the values near the center of a distribution.

Concept: An idea of interest, or utility.

Confidence Interval: As used in this book, the interval that includes all values within a specific standard deviation of the mean. For instance, the "confidence interval for mean at 95% level" refers to the interval that extends 1.96 SDs on either side of the sample mean. The reasoning is that in the long run, 95 percent of such calculated intervals would encompass the population mean, and 5 percent would not. Whether the particular interval calculated is one of the 95 percent is a calculated risk.

Construct: A concept adopted for a scientific purpose.

Content Analysis: Analysis of any of various communication phenomena, e.g., word count, subject matter determination, changes, trends, and so on. It is, in effect, a method of data collection as well.

Control Card: A punched card used to control subsequent operations of a computer by communicating instructions to the machine.

Control Group: A group used for comparison with another group.

Conversational Mode: Input to a computer in small units of a continuing program and receiving immediate output as a response to each input. *Batch Mode* as an antonym.

Critical Value: One value of a series of such values, such that subsequent operations are changed.

CPU: Central processing unit. On a computer printout, it indicates the time period that the program occupied the attention of the CPU for billing purposes.

Data Deck: A set of punched cards containing data relevant to subject matter, as differentiated from "control deck," which conveys instructions about what to do with the data.

Deck: A set of computer cards punched with information, coded in a sequence of punched holes.

Degrees of Freedom: The number of values that are free to vary, after certain restrictions have been placed on the data. The quality of an estimate varies as the number of the degrees of freedom.

Derived Score: Scores derived from raw data values to facilitate a researcher's purpose, e.g., to compare standings of individuals in different-sized groups. See Appendix D for one type.

Deviation: Deviation of a score from the mean of that distribution:

$$x = X - \overline{X}$$

where $\overline{X}$ = mean
X = score

Documentation: Supporting records to prove the organization of input and output. Can be written or graphic or both. If for a computer, prepared at the time it is written. Useful to locate "bugs."

Error Statement: A computer printout that states or describes an error.

Experimental Group: A group being studied, about which it is sought to control all influencing variables.

Factor Analysis: A multivariate analysis whose purpose is to identify influencing variables.

F-distribution: A family of theoretical distributions. Often used to test hypotheses regarding variability of samples.

Flowchart: Pictorial analysis of an operation.

FORTRAN: A programming language adapted to scientific applications, that is, small amounts of input and output, but with large amounts of calculation. Source of name: FORmula TRANslation.

Function: A mathematical quantity whose value depends on the value of other quantities, called the independent variables of the function.

GIGO: Abbreviation for "garbage in, garbage out." refers to the fact that if inaccurate data or improper instructions are input into a computer, the output will be useless.

Graph: A diagram showing a system of interrelations among two or more elements.

H_0: The null hypothesis; a denial that the expected relationship exists. It states that any observed incidence of an apparent relationship is no greater than should be expected by chance.

H_1: Here used to refer to the statistical hypothesis; an operationalization in measurable form of the substantive hypothesis. The hypothesis that will be tentatively accepted if H_0 is rejected.

Histogram: A graph of a frequency distribution in which, when manually drawn, equal intervals of values are scaled on a horizontal axis, and the frequency corresponding to each interval is indicated by the height of a rectangle having the interval as its base. Computer-printed histograms may vary in style for technical reasons. In every case, however, it is important to note the relative position of zero along both axes, lest an error in judgment be made when estimating the scores graphed.

Hypothesis: Tentative or conjectural solution to a problem. If stated in testable form, it is often called a substantive or scientific hypothesis. Invariably it can be stated in if-*A*-then-*B* form (q.v.), i.e., a relation between two or more variables. If the hypothesis is expressed in quantitative terms, it is called a statistical hypothesis, and symbolized in this book as H_1 (q.v.).

If A then B: Statement of a proposed relationship between two variables. There is a group of synonyms for the *A* variable that cannot be interchanged in a given if-*A*-then-*B* statement with a similar set of synonyms for the *B* variable. That is, the relationship is not deemed necessarily reversible, although on occasion that may be the case and can be so indicated in another statement. To summarize the usage:

A variables	B variables
Independent variable	Dependent variable
Stimulus variable	Response variable
Treatment variable	Effect variable
Experimental variable	Criterion variable
Manipulated variable	Measured variable
Active variable	Attribute variable
Controlled variable	Consequent variable
Predictor variable	Predicted variable
x variable	y variable

The synonyms in one column are often used interchangeably with one another. Different disciplines have a tendency to use some more often than others, e.g., psychology tends to use "stimulus and response" variables. In the case of the use of x and y to indicate the independent and dependent variables, the "then" relationship is usually written in reverse sequence: $y = f(x)$, or "y is a function of x," indicating that the magnitude of y *depends* on the magnitude of x. "Then" signifies any relationship whatever that may be specified; a tie, or connection; or a set of ordered pairs of attributes.

μ: Generally used symbol for the population-mean.

Machine Language: The language that a computer "understands" without needing a compiler. The manufacturer of the computer supplies with it a special set of programs called "compilers," which translate English-like program languages such as FORTRAN and COBOL into machine language.

Mean: Arithmetic mean (q.v.) is what is usually meant. Actually there are many other kinds of mathematical terms referred to as "mean"—geometric, harmonic, contraharmonic, and other means. When "mean" is used without further description, however, it is taken to refer to the arithmetic mean.

Median: The central value of a set of score-values; the fiftieth percentile; or the average of the two most nearly central values if there is an even number of score-values.

Memory: Term applied to the ability of a computer to store data and instructions until they are called for.

Mode: The most frequent score-value.

Multiple Regression Analysis: A multivariate analysis that tries to discover the effect that two or more independent variables have on dependent variables.

Multivariate Analysis: The analysis of many independent and dependent variables simultaneously. The if-A-then-B model can be used to include these functional relationships in discussion.

N: Total number of scores or quantities.

Natural Language: Communication similar to that used by humans. Often used improperly to describe the English-like qualities of programming languages such as COBOL or FORTRAN.

Nonparametric Test: A test that does not specify parameters of the population from which the sample is drawn, e.g., without assumption of a normal shape to the distribution.

Normal Curve: A bell-shaped freuqency curve with a specific mathematical formula. Called "normal" because the distribution of many population attributes of living organisms has been observed to approximate this curve quite closely. See Table H-1 and Figures 6-1 and 6-2.

OFFLINE: Not directly connected to a computer, e.g., punched card machines or card-to-tape readers.

ONE-TAILED TEST: Rejection of H_0 when the test-finding falls into one of the tails of low frequency of the distribution used for comparison.

ONLINE: Connected always directly to the computer as an input or output device. Contrasted with "OFFLINE."

$p(A)$: Probability of event A.

$P(B|A)$: Probability of event B, given that A has already occurred.

Packaged Program: A system of programs that can direct a computer to perform a related set of procedures with a minimum of human intervention. Often used to simplify the use of the computer to perform statistical computations.

Parameter: A variable whose value affects the form of a distribution. Often used to refer to a population-value as distinguished from a statistic, which in this sense would refer to a sample-value.

Pearson Product-Moment Correlation Coefficient: A correlation coefficient, one of many. This one provides an accurate measure of the degree of association between two variables *if* the interval or higher measurement is appropriate, and the actual relationship is linear (not a curve).

Percentile: One of the values of a variable that divides the frequency distribution into 100 groups having equal frequencies.

Population: Entire set of a given attribute. Statistics for population values are usually symbolized by Greek letters, e.g., σ for standard deviation, μ for population mean.

Program: A record of each sequential step of a procedure designed to communicate with a computer. The record can be a typed or handwritten listing for later translation, or, made directly on a computer keyboard on punched cards, magnetic tape, drum, or other means. A program, once properly set up and tested, may be applied to many different sets of data with only minor adjustments.

Program Language: A communication code of symbols and syntax designed to communicate with a computer.

Range: The absolute difference between the maximum and minimum values. It is the simplest measure of variation, and when there are only two scores, it uses all the data has to tell. However, when there are many scores, it ignores much information contained in the data.

Regression Line: Line representing the functional relationship between two or more values. Often deduceable from a scattering of observations intuitively, by various statistical procedures, or by a computer.

σ: Symbol for the standard deviation (SD) of a population.

$$\sigma = \sqrt{\frac{\Sigma (X - \overline{X})^2}{N}}$$

The population standard deviation is often unknown.

s: Symbol often used for the standard deviation (SD) of a sample, as an *estimate* of the population SD.

$$s = \sqrt{\frac{\Sigma (X - \overline{X})^2}{N-1}}$$

N.B.: The denominator is $N-1$ because there are $N-1$ degrees of freedom. The number of degrees of freedom is the number of variables. The number of degrees of freedom is reduced by one for each restriction— that is, for each statistic computed from the sample—and used as an estimate of a parameter. The use of a sample value as an estimate of a population value reduces the number of degrees of freedom by one.)

Scattergram, also Scatterplot: A graphic representation that shows type and degree of relation between two variables.

Significant: Statistically important under the rules set up for the particular analysis. Thus "significant at the .05 level" means that the obtained result may be expected to occur by chance 5 times in 100 trials, in the long run, based on a normal distribution. Another way of saying this is: 95 percent of a normal distribution would be between +1.96 and −1.96 standard deviations of the arithmetic mean, and that the observation falls within those limits.

SPSS: Statistical Package for the Social Sciences. A packaged program consisting of a system of programs offering to automate and routinize data analysis required by social scientists. As of 1976, it is a batch process only, not being available in conversational mode. Developed at Stanford University, it is published by McGraw-Hill.

Standard Deviation: See *s.*

Standard Error of Mean: A measure of the stability of the mean. The potential degree of discrepancy between the sample mean and the (usually) unknown population mean. Specifically, it is the standard deviation of a sampling distribution of the means, were an infinite number of samples to be drawn. Symbolically:

$$\sigma_M = \frac{\sigma}{\sqrt{N}}$$

Standard Scores: Usually refers to z-scores, or a derivative called *T*-scores (q.v.), which measure score distances from the mean of a distribution in units of the standard deviation of that distribution.

Statistic: A measure calculated from a large number of values, and summarizing or describing them as a group.

Statistical Test: A comparison of empirically observed results with those to be expected, usually on the basis of chance, e.g., levels of significance; confidence intervals; statistical estimation, and various probability approaches.

STATJOB: A statistical packaged program designed to automate and routinize data analysis. Developed by the Madison Computer Center and published by Sperry-Rand, it is designed particularly for the Univac series of computers.

Studentized Mean: The arithmetic mean divided by the standard error of the mean.

Student's t: Also known as *t*-distribution. A theoretical distribution used to test hypotheses about an unknown population mean. It is symmetrical about zero, like the normal distribution, but it has more of a peak for small sample sizes. As the sample grows larger, the *t*-distribution approaches the normal shape. It is often used to test hypotheses about mean differences and correlations.

t-distribution: See *Student's t.*

Time-sharing: Simultaneous use of a computer by many users via separate input/output terminals.

T-score: A derivative of the z-score consisting entirely of positive values. Calculated by multiplying the *z*-score value (i.e., standard deviations) by 10, rounding off to nearest whole number, and adding 50. Thus the mean of a distribution of *T*-scores must be 50, and its standard deviation must be 10.

Two-tailed Test: Rejection of H_0 when the test-finding falls into either of the two tails of low frequency of the distribution used for comparison with the sample-values observed.

Type I Error: See α.

Type II Error: See β.

Univariate Analysis: The analysis of a single variable as to when and how it is distributed, e.g., a frequency distribution.

Variance: The average of the squared deviations from the mean; the square of the standard deviation.

VDU: Visual Display Unit [or visual display terminal or cathode ray tube (CRT)] : Device used to display on a cathode ray tube the input and output of a computer.

z: Deviation of a specific score from the mean, expressed in units of the standard deviation of that group $z = \dfrac{X - \overline{X}}{s}$. See Appendix H. Also known as *z*-score.

$Z_{0.05} = \pm 1.96$: Symbolizes the minimum value of Z required to reject H_0 at the 0.05 level of significance, two-tailed test. The computer can only print out upper case letters thus the presence of a capital Z when lower case z would be used in ordinary printing or typing.

Appendix H:
How to Use Standard Scores:
z-Scores and T-scores

Standard scores can be used to compare individual standings in relation to their different groups. The examples given in Chapter 5 of the relative heights of Watusi, American, and Japanese officers in their respective groups are quite obvious instances where standard scores would be useful. Actually, standard scores are merely measures of standings in terms of the standard deviation of that group from its mean.

As an examination of Figure 6-2 shows, if an individual raw score is transformed into a z-score of, say, +2, he will be among the 4 percent of individuals who are his height or taller, *if* height is normally distributed among that group. This would be so whether or not the height-attribute scores grouped very closely around a central mean value or not (see Figure 6-1).

The normal curve fixes the ordered pairs of z-score and corresponding percentile. The line of the normal curve and the tabled paired values of z and percentile in Tables H-1 and H-2 are merely different ways of saying the same thing. The percentile rank of a z-score is the percent of z-scores below it; it is invariable in the normal curve.

As more or less distance is allotted horizontally along the axis for the z-value, or along the vertical axis for the frequencies involved in a particular normal curve, the shape may appear to change, but the relationship between each percentile and its corresponding z remains the same.

By definition, a standard score is the number of standard deviations above or below the mean that the raw score is located, or

$$z = \frac{X - \overline{X}}{SD}$$

where X = raw score
       $\overline{X}$ = mean
       SD = standard deviation.

That is, raw scores are changed into z-scores by subtracting the mean and dividing by the standard deviation. Since the mean and the standard deviation are in the same units as the raw score, the ratio that is the z-score is simply the number of times the standard deviation "goes into" the distance from the mean.

For example, what is the probability that a randomly chosen candidate from the general population will be 6 feet tall or over? Empirical evidence indicates that the heights of the general population arrange themselves into a normal distribution, with a mean of 68 inches and a standard deviation of 3

Table H-1

Normal Curve Areas to Left of z-Score

(z-Score Paired with Percentile Rank)

−4.0	0.000	−1.3	0.097	1.4	0.919
−3.9	.000	−1.2	.115	1.5	.933
−3.8	.000	−1.1	.136	1.6	.945
−3.7	.00C	−1.0	.159	1.7	.955
−3.6	.000	−0.9	.184	1.8	.964
−3.5	.000	−0.8	.212	1.9	.971
−3.4	.000	−0.7	.242	2.0	.977
−3.3	.001	−0.6	.274	2.1	.982
−3.2	.001	−0.5	.308	2.2	.986
−3.1	.001	−0.4	.345	2.3	.989
−3.0	.001	−0.3	.382	2.4	.992
−2.9	.002	−0.2	.421	2.5	.994
−2.8	.003	−0.1	.460	2.6	.995
−2.7	.004	0.0	.500	2.7	.996
−2.6	.005	0.1	.540	2.8	.997
−2.5	.006	0.2	.579	2.9	.998
−2.4	.008	0.3	.618	3.0	.999
−2.3	.011	0.4	.655	3.1	.999
−2.2	.014	0.5	.692	3.2	.999
−2.1	.018	0.6	.726	3.3	.999
−2.0	.023	0.7	.758	3.4	1.000
−1.9	.029	0.8	.788	3.5	1.000
−1.8	.036	0.9	.816	3.6	1.000
−1.7	.045	1.0	.841	3.7	1.000
−1.6	.055	1.1	.864	3.8	1.000
−1.5	.067	1.2	.885	3.9	1.000
−1.4	0.081	1.3	0.903	4.0	1.000

Note: The above frequency distribution can also be expressed:

$$Y = f = \frac{N}{\sigma\sqrt{2\pi}} \exp \frac{1}{2} \left(\frac{X - \mu}{\sigma} \right)^2$$

where exp = 2.71813. The glossary explains the meaning of the other terms.

inches. Six feet, or 72 inches, is 4 inches more than the mean. The distance from the mean, 4 inches, divided by the 3 inches of standard deviation is a 1.33 z-score.

By noting this z-score's position on the normal curve of Figure 6-2, one can see that the chance of randomly picking a candidate is less than 15.8 percent, because it falls into the part of the curve's area that represents that part of the entire expected distribution. Verifying the figure with Table H-1 gives a more precise answer less than 9.7%.

One can argue that there are a great number of 6-foot officers in the department, and the chance of picking one must be much greater than 10 percent. But the population is *not* the general public. The officers have been selected, or have selected themselves, by conditions that give a non-normal distribution. Empirical evidence does not reveal that the mean height of officers is 5 feet, 8 inches, as is the general population. If an administrator wants officers either taller or shorter than the general population, he cannot depend on random selection from the public.

An even more interesting use of standard scores is to determine the probability that a sample will be representative of the population from which it is drawn. This is illustrated by trying to determine the population mean of an attribute.

A random sample of the attribute is drawn to measure the arithmetic mean of that sample. Since we know (from the Central Limit Theorem) that in the long run such sample-means will take a normal distribution, a second sample drawn, and its mean measured, will give a figure that can be compared with the first sample-mean, to determine the probability that the second sample will be within the bounds of a numbered probability of being of the same population.

This is simply done as follows: The first sample-mean and sample-standard deviation are presumed to be identical to the unknown population-mean and population standard deviation. The second sample's raw score is transformed into a z-score, and where it falls on the normal curve is noted. The percentage of the area of the curve that is within that z-score distance from the mean is a numbered probability that the second sample will be of the same population.

If, for instance, the second sample z-score is -1, it is clear that a bit more than 68 percent of such samples would be within that distance of the mean, and 32 percent of the means would fall outside that mark. If the second sample had been "treated" with an independent variable, one could say that 68 percent of the samples even without treatment would have shown that much change. Is the result "significant"? No, not in ordinary statistical terms, which generally use the word "significant" if the sample falls into the area of the curve indicating that only 5 percent or less of such samples would show such a result in a normal chance distribution, i.e., a level of significance of .05.

It is often helpful to be able to calculate the values of the areas between the rounded-off z-scores of the graphed curve. Tables H-1 and H-2 give more exact values than can be visually scaled off the graph. The tables do more exactly what is done by visual estimation. Of course, even the tables are incomplete, and do not give all possible z-scores and areas, for these values are both *continuous*. The numbered values in the table are categorical. There are larger tables, with more listings. Or the values could be defined more precisely by the use of still another measure, or language, called the calculus.

The T-score can be used in the same way as the z-score, for it is merely a further transformation of the z-score itself. The advantage of the T-score is that the elimination of decimals and minus signs reduces the proclivity to error at the human interface in data handling.

Table H-2
Normal Curve Areas from Mean to z-Score

z	0.00	0.01	0.02	0.03	0.04	0.05
0.0	0.0000	0.0040	0.0080	0.0120	0.0160	0.0199
0.1	.0398	.0438	.0478	.0517	.0557	.0596
0.2	.0793	.0832	.0871	.0910	.0948	.0987
0.3	.1179	.1217	.1255	.1293	.1331	.1368
0.4	.1554	.1591	.1628	.1664	.1700	.1736
0.5	.1915	.1950	.1985	.2019	.2054	.2088
0.6	.2257	.2291	.2324	.2357	.2389	.2422
0.7	.2580	.2611	.2642	.2673	.2704	.2734
0.8	.2881	.2910	.2939	.2967	.2995	.3023
0.9	.3159	.3186	.3212	.3238	.3264	.3289
1.0	.3413	.3438	.3461	.3485	.3508	.3531
1.1	.3643	.3665	.3686	.3708	.3729	.3749
1.2	.3849	.3869	.3888	.3907	.3925	.3944
1.3	.4032	.4049	.4066	.4082	.4099	.4115
1.4	.4192	.4207	.4222	.4236	.4251	.4265
1.5	.4332	.4345	.4357	.4370	.4382	.4394
1.6	.4452	.4463	.4474	.4484	.4495	.4505
1.7	.4554	.4564	.4573	.4582	.4591	.4599
1.8	.4641	.4649	.4656	.4664	.4671	.4678
1.9	.4713	.4719	.4726	.4732	.4738	.4744
2.0	.4772	.4778	.4783	.4788	.4793	.4798
2.1	.4821	.4826	.4830	.4834	.4838	.4842
2.2	.4861	.4864	.4868	.4871	.4875	.4878
2.3	.4893	.4896	.4898	.4901	.4904	.4906
2.4	.4918	.4920	.4922	.4925	.4927	.4929
2.5	.4938	.4940	.4941	.4943	.4945	.4946
2.6	.4953	.4955	.4956	.4957	.4959	.4960
2.7	.4965	.4966	.4967	.4968	.4969	.4970
2.8	.4974	.4975	.4976	.4977	.4977	.4978
2.9	.4981	.4982	.4982	.4983	.4984	.4984
3.0	.4987	0.4987	0.4987	0.4988	0.4988	0.4989
3.1	.49903					
3.2	.49931					
3.3	.49952					
3.4	.49966					
3.5	.49977					
3.6	.49984					
3.7	.49989					
3.8	.49993					
3.9	.49995					
4.0	0.50000					

149

0.06	0.07	0.08	0.09
0.0239	0.0279	0.0319	0.0359
.0636	.0675	.0714	.0753
.1026	.1064	.1103	.1141
.1406	.1443	.1480	.1517
.1772	.1808	.1844	.1879
.2123	.2157	.2190	.2224
.2454	.2486	.2517	.2549
.2764	.2794	.2823	.2852
.3051	.3078	.3106	.3133
.3315	.3340	.3365	.3389
.3554	.3577	.3599	.3621
.3770	.3790	.3810	.3830
.3962	.3980	.3997	.4015
.4131	.4147	.4162	.4177
.4279	.4292	.4306	.4319
.4406	.4418	.4429	.4441
.4515	.4525	.4535	.4545
.4608	.4616	.4625	.4633
.4686	.4693	.4699	.4706
.4750	.4756	.4761	.4767
.4803	.4808	.4812	.4817
.4846	.4850	.4854	.4857
.4881	.4884	.4887	.4890
.4909	.4911	.4913	.4916
.4931	.4932	.4934	.4936
.4948	.4949	.4951	.4952
.4961	.4962	.4963	.4964
.4971	.4972	.4973	.4974
.4979	.4979	.4980	.4981
.4985	.4985	.4986	.4986
0.4989	0.4989	0.4990	0.4990

To transform z-scores into T-scores, the procedure is to multiply z by 10, round off to nearest whole number, and then add 50.

The only conceivable way the T-score could be negative would be if the z-value were less than −5.0. Examination of Figure 6-2 shows that the probability is so remote as to be negligible. In fact, Table H-1 and H-2 both completely ignore it, as being so unlikely that it would never be encountered in the practical world of research.

If a curve other than the normal is deemed more appropriate to the particular distribution of concern, then that curve and standard deviation units can be used as a measure. Of course, however, the percentiles corresponding to each standard deviation unit will be different than in the normal curve.

For illustrative purposes the curve known as the t-distribution is presented in Table H-3. Note that (1) t-distribution curves have *no* connection with T-scores, and (2) t-curves are different for each difference in the degrees of freedom of the standard deviation (q.v. in the glossary). Therefore with small samples the curve of t is quite a bit different from the normal. However, with larger samples the t-curve approaches very nearly the normal shape.

Table H-3
t-Curve Areas to Left of t-Value Listed at Top of Columns

d.f.	0.005	0.010	0.025	0.050	0.500	0.950	0.975	0.990	0.995
1	-63.66	-31.82	-12.71	-6.31	0.00	6.31	12.71	31.82	63.66
2	-9.92	-6.96	-4.30	-2.92	0.00	2.92	4.30	6.96	9.92
3	-5.84	-4.54	-3.18	-2.35	0.00	2.35	3.18	4.54	5.84
4	-4.60	-3.75	-2.78	-2.13	0.00	2.13	2.78	3.75	4.60
5	-4.03	-3.36	-2.57	-2.02	0.00	2.02	2.57	3.36	4.03
6	-3.71	-3.14	-2.45	-1.94	0.00	1.94	2.45	3.14	3.71
7	-3.50	-3.00	-2.36	-1.90	0.00	1.90	2.36	3.00	3.50
8	-3.36	-2.90	-2.31	-1.86	0.00	1.86	2.31	2.90	3.36
9	-3.25	-2.82	-2.26	-1.83	0.00	1.83	2.26	2.82	3.25
10	-3.17	-2.76	-2.23	-1.81	0.00	1.81	2.23	2.76	3.17
11	-3.11	-2.72	-2.20	-1.80	0.00	1.80	2.20	2.72	3.11
12	-3.06	-2.68	-2.18	-1.78	0.00	1.78	2.18	2.68	3.06
13	-3.01	-2.65	-2.16	-1.77	0.00	1.77	2.16	2.65	3.01
14	-2.98	-2.62	-2.14	-1.76	0.00	1.76	2.14	2.62	2.98
15	-2.95	-2.60	-2.13	-1.75	0.00	1.75	2.13	2.60	2.95
16	-2.92	-2.58	-2.12	-1.75	0.00	1.75	2.12	2.58	2.92
17	-2.90	-2.57	-2.11	-1.74	0.00	1.74	2.11	2.57	2.90
18	-2.88	-2.55	-2.10	-1.73	0.00	1.73	2.10	2.55	2.88
19	-2.86	-2.54	-2.09	-1.73	0.00	1.73	2.09	2.54	2.86
20	-2.84	-2.53	-2.09	-1.72	0.00	1.72	2.09	2.53	2.84
21	-2.83	-2.52	-2.08	-1.72	0.00	1.72	2.08	2.52	2.83
22	-2.82	-2.51	-2.07	-1.72	0.00	1.72	2.07	2.51	2.82
23	-2.81	-2.50	-2.07	-1.71	0.00	1.71	2.07	2.50	2.81
24	-2.80	-2.49	-2.06	-1.71	0.00	1.71	2.06	2.49	2.80
25	-2.79	-2.48	-2.06	-1.71	0.00	1.71	2.06	2.48	2.79
26	-2.78	-2.48	-2.06	-1.71	0.00	1.71	2.06	2.48	2.78
27	-2.77	-2.47	-2.05	-1.70	0.00	1.70	2.05	2.47	2.77
28	-2.76	-2.47	-2.05	-1.70	0.00	1.70	2.05	2.47	2.76

Table H-3 (cont.)

d.f.	0.005	0.010	0.025	0.050	0.500	0.950	0.975	0.990	0.995
29	-2.76	-2.46	-2.04	-1.70	0.00	1.70	2.04	2.46	2.76
30	-2.75	-2.46	-2.04	-1.70	0.00	1.70	2.04	2.46	2.75
31	-2.75	-2.45	-2.04	-1.70	0.00	1.70	2.04	2.45	2.75
32	-2.74	-2.45	-2.03	-1.69	0.00	1.69	2.03	2.45	2.74
33	-2.74	-2.45	-2.03	-1.69	0.00	1.69	2.03	2.45	2.74

t-values are in the body of this table.

d.f. = degrees of freedom (see glossary).

Note: t-values are *not* T-scores, which are derived from Z-scores, and refer only to the normal curve.

Source: Abridged from Table III of Fisher and Yates: *Statistical Tables for Biological, Agricultural and Medical Research*, published by Longman Group Ltd., London (previously published by Oliver and Boyd, Edinburgh), and by permission of the authors and publishers.

Notes

Notes

Chapter 1
The Professional in a World of Research

1. "Justice" is changing its meaning to the professional in criminal justice. Where once the "law of the nightstick" was acceptable as the "just" way to handle rowdies and habitual criminals, now such discretionary street-side resolutions are intolerable. See Jerome Skolnick, *Justice Without Trial: Law Enforcement in a Democratic Society* (New York: Wiley, 1967); and Paul Chevigny, "The Right to Resist An Unlawful Arrest," *The Yale Law Journal* 78, no. 7 (1969):1128-1150.

2. The general acceptance of the practice of police-administered punishment as a curb on lawlessness was a decades-old institution by the 1930s. The National Commission on Law Observance and Enforcement, in its *Report on Lawlessness in Law Enforcement*, no. 11 (Washington, D.C.: U.S. Government Printing Office, 1931), documented the widespread use of the "third degree" as an enforcement tool that met with wide approval when used against gangsters and violent criminals. This viewpoint is contrasted with the President's Commission on Law Enforcement and Administration of Justice's *Task Force Report: The Police* (Washington, D.C.: U.S. Government Printing Office, 1967), which harshly condemns even the overnight detention of practicing prostitutes (p. 187).

3. See Lawrence W. Sherman, "The Sociology and the Social Reform of the American Police: 1950-1973," paper presented at the Second Nuffield Seminar on the Sociology of the Police, University of Bristol, April 1973, which details twenty-three years of sociological interventions; I. Piliavin and S. Briar, "Police Encounters with Juveniles," *American Journal of Sociology* 70 (1965):206-214; J. Chwast, "Value Conflicts in Law Enforcement," *Crime and Delinquency* II (1965):151; Egon Bittner, *The Functions of Police in Modern Society* (Bethesda, Md.: National Institute of Mental Health, 1970); Georgette Bennett Sandler and Ellen Mintz, "Police Organizations: Their Changing Internal and External Relationships," *Journal of Police Science and Administration* 2, no. 4 (1974):458-463.

Lewis A. Coser, *The Functions of Social Conflict* (New York: The Free Press, 1956), fails of providing experimental data; as does D. McGregor, "The Human Side of Enterprise," in David R. Hampton, ed., *Behavioral Concepts in Management*, 2nd ed. (Encino, Calif.: Dickenson Publishing Co., 1972), pp. 8-18. These humanistic concepts contrast with B.F. Skinner's ominous view of a necessary future in *Beyond Freedom and Dignity* (New York: Bantam/Vintage, 1972), which calls for an equally new, but oppositely oriented, criminal justice structure and process. More rigorous approaches, but still unconvincing to

155

practitioners in both police and correctional services, are the implications of Albert K. Cohen and James F. Short, Jr. in "Crime and Juvenile Delinquency," in Robert K. Merton and Robert Nisbet, eds., *Contemporary Social Problems*, 3rd ed. (New York: Harcourt Brace Jovanovich, 1971), pp. 89-146.

4. E.M. Davis, "The Gordian Knot," *The Police Chief*, 43, no. 4 (1976):18-22. Chief Davis, of the Los Angeles Police Department, suggests, "The control of criminal justice planning boards at the state and local level must be taken out of the hands of politicians and returned to the criminal justice practitioners" (p. 22).

See also Richard Block and David J. Ross, "Theory, Method and Program Success: A Computer Assisted Technique for Analyzing and Summarizing Delinquency Prevention Program," a report for the Urban Institute, Washington, D.C., reprinted in Emilio Viano, ed., *Criminal Justice Research* (Lexington, Mass.: Lexington Books, D.C. Heath, 1975), pp. 219-234; and the Rand report that suggests that detective duty can and perhaps should be performed by uniformed patrol officers: P.W. Greenwood and J. Petersilia, *The Criminal Investigation Process*, 3 vols. (Santa Monica, Calif.: Rand, 1975). A short comment on the Kansas City Preventive Patrol Experiment that has received favorable comment from both sides of the discussion is R.S. Clark, "Guidelines in Research," in *The Police Chief* (June 1976), p. 83.

5. For a general discussion, see George Counts, "The Impact of Technological Change," in Warren G. Bennis, Kenneth D. Benne, and Robert Chin, eds., *The Planning of Change* (New York: Holt, Rinehart & Winston, 1964), pp. 20-28.

6. Colin Cherry, *On Human Communication* (Cambridge, Mass.: MIT Press, 1970), p. 2.

7. See Alex C. Michalos, *Principles of Logic* (Englewood Cliffs, N.J.: Prentice-Hall, 1969), pp. 181 ff.

8. The dynamics of the controller of information in structuring reality is discussed in another, but relevant, context by Franklin Fearing, "Human Communication," in L.A. Dexter and D.M. White, eds., *People, Society and Mass Communication* (New York: The Free Press, 1964), pp. 37-68.

Information research appears to reach for its ultimate rationale in mathematical concepts. Cherry, *On Human Communication*, pp. 41 ff. is a relatively simple introduction to this interesting study.

For a more advanced text, see C.E. Shannon and W. Weaver, *The Mathematical Theory of Communication* (Urbana: University of Illinois Press, 1949).

9. Elmer Sprague and Paul W. Taylor, eds., *Knowledge and Value* (New York: Harcourt Brace, 1959), p. 174. The authors' comment, "The scientific notion of proof involves an appeal to sense experience" reveals that even scientific approaches submit themselves to the flaws inherent in empiricism (see note 10).

10. George H. Weinberg and John A. Schumaker, *Statistics: An Intuitive Approach*, 3rd ed. (Monterey, Calif.: Brooks/Cole, 1974). Suggests skepticism as a proper response to the dangers cited in note 9.

11. Claire Selltiz, M. Jahoda, M. Deutsch, and S. Cook, *Research Methods in Social Relations* (New York: Holt, Rinehart & Winston, 1961), pp. 46-47.

12. Donald T. Campbell, "Factors Relevant to the Validity of Experiments in Social Settings," in Carl W. Backman and Paul F. Secord, eds., *Problems in Social Psychology* (New York: McGraw-Hill, 1966). See also Donald T. Campbell and Julian C. Stanley, *Experimental and Quasi-Experimental Designs for Research* (Chicago: Rand McNally, 1966).

13. Fred N. Kerlinger, *Foundations of Behavioral Research*, 2nd ed. (New York: Holt, Rinehart & Winston, 1973), p. 20.

14. The system of notation developed in this work, of which the if-A-then-B statement is a part, is from Moritz Schlick, "Causality in Everyday Life and in Recent Science," in *Publications in Philosophy* vol. 15 (Berkeley: University of California Press, 1932). See also, J. Dewey, *How We Think* (Boston, Mass.: D.C. Heath, 1933).

15. Daniel E. Bailey, *Probability and Statistics* (New York: Wiley, 1971), pp. 286-287.

16. Bailey, on p. 257 ff., discusses in relatively simple form the philosophy of probabilistic statements. Lyman G. Parratt, *Probability and Experimental Errors in Science* (New York: Dover, 1961), points out that "Probability is the lens that brings science into philosophic focus" (p. vii), and suggests that probability should be studied separately from mathematics and statistics, as the unifying subject in all science. A. Papoulis, in *Probability, Random Variables and Stochastic Processes* (New York: McGraw-Hill, 1965), agrees (p. 4).

17. M. Polanyi, in *Personal Knowledge* (Chicago: University of Chicago Press, 1958) points out that the hypothesis is an attempt to reach beyond the reseacher's own bias and personality (p. 4).

18. Kerlinger, in *Foundations of Behavioral Research*, states that "scientists systematically and consciously use the self-corrective aspect of the scientific approach," which implies the cyclic feedback of new conclusions into new hypotheses and data collection, to findings and back to conclusions, round and round again, with no forseeable end (p. 6).

Chapter Two
Scientific Inquiry into Criminal Justice

1. See President's Commission on Law Enforcement and Administration of Justice, *Task Force Report: The Police* (Washington, D.C.: U.S. Government Printing Office, 1967), p. 37, which says, "modern information systems can greatly assist the police . . . and provide the basis for both short and long range

research." See also Richard W. Brightman, *Information Systems for Modern Management* (New York: Macmillan, 1971), pp. 4-5.

2. R. Kershner and L. Wilcox, *The Anatomy of Mathematics* (New York, Ronald, 1950), p. 35; and J. Piaget, *Logic and Thinking* (New York: Basic Books, 1957).

3. Fred N. Kerlinger, *Foundations of Behavioral Research*, 2nd ed. (New York: Holt, Rinehart & Winston, 1973), p. 178.

4. S. Siegel, *Nonparametric Statistics* (New York: McGraw-Hill, 1956); E.P. Hickman and J.G. Hilton, *Probability and Statistical Analysis* (London: Intext Educational, 1971), pp. 46 ff; and Daniel E. Bailey, *Probability and Statistics* (New York: Wiley, 1971), pp. 45 ff., esp. p. 60.

5. Brightman, *Information Systems*, pp. 67-68.

6. Report of the President's Commission on Law Enforcement and Administration of Justice, *Task Force Report: The Police* (Washington, D.C.: U.S. Government Printing Office, 1967), pp. 13-15; J.V. Vandiver, "Acquisition and Disposition of Police Front Line Information," *Journal of Police Science and Administration* 2, no. 3 (1974):288-296.

7. Egon Bittner, *The Functions of the Police in Modern Society* (Washington, D.C.: National Institute of Mental Health, 1970).

8. E. Greenwood, "The Practice of Science and the Science of Practice," in Warren G. Bennis, Kenneth D. Benne, and Robert Chin, eds., *The Planning of Change* (New York: Holt, Rinehart & Winston, 1964), pp. 74-75.

9. P.M. Whisenand and R.F. Ferguson, *The Managing of Police Organizations* (Englewood Cliffs, N.J.: Prentice-Hall, 1973), p. 1.

10. Alex C. Michalos, *Principles of Logic* (Englewood Cliffs, N.J.: Prentice-Hall, 1969), p. 1, quoting John Stuart Mill, "The only complete safeguard against reasoning ill, is the habit of reasoning well."

11. Warren G. Bennis, Kenneth D. Benne, and Robert Chin, "Conceptual Tools for the Change Agent: Social System and Change Models," in *The Planning of Change* (New York: Holt, Rinehart & Winston, 1964), pp. 187-200, esp. p. 191.

12. Lyman G. Parratt, *Probability and Experimental Errors in Science* (New York: Dover, 1961), p. 239.

13. Donald W. Taylor, "Decision Making and Problem Solving," in James G. March, ed., *Handbook of Organizations* (Chicago: Rand McNally, 1965), pp. 72-75.

14. Morris R. Cohen and Ernest Nagel, *An Introduction to Logic and Scientific Method* (New York: Harcourt, Brace 1936), Chapter 11, "Hypotheses and Scientific Method."

15. D.R. Weidman, J.D. Waller, D. MacNeil, F.L. Tolson, and J.S. Wholey, *Intensive Evaluation for Criminal Justice Planning Agencies* (Washington, D.C.:

LEAA/NILECJ, 1975), p. 3. See also *LEAA Guideline Manual*, M4100.1C CHG 1, U.S. Department of Justice, Law Enforcement Assistance Administration, November 1, 1974.

16. H.P. Hatry, R.E. Winnie, and D.M. Fisk, *Practical Program Evaluation for State and Local Government Officials* (Washington, D.C.: The Urban Institute, 1973).

Chapter 3
Research Design

1. G.C. Helmstedter, "Common Errors in the Design of Research Studies in the Behavioral Sciences," in *Research Concepts in Human Behavior* (New York: Meredith, 1970), pp. 121-127. See also, D.R. Weidman, J.D. Waller, D. MacNeil, F.L. Tolson, and J.S. Wholey, *Intensive Evaluation for Criminal Justice Planning Agencies* (Washington, D.C.: LEAA/NILECJ, 1975), pp. 1-3.

2. Academic Research Information System, *Social and Natural Science Report* (San Francisco, August 1976).

3. Donald T. Campbell and Julian C. Stanley, *Experimental and Quasi-Experimental Designs for Research* (Chicago: Rand McNally, 1966).

4. N. Wiener, *I Am a Mathematician* (New York: Doubleday, 1956), pp. 302-303.

5. H.W. Smith, *Strategies of Social Research* (Englewood Cliffs, N.J.: Prentice-Hall, 1975), Chapter 1, "Ethical Commitments in Social and Behavioral Research" (pp. 3-5).

6. Ibid., pp. 5-17.

7. R. Fisher, *The Design of Experiments*, 6th ed. (New York: Hafner, 1951).

8. D. Stilson, *Probability and Statistics in Psychological Research and Theory* (San Francisco: Holden-Day, 1966).

9. R.D. Luce, R.R. Bush and E. Galanter, eds., *Handbook of Mathematical Psychology* (New York: Wiley, 1963), pp. 191-243; and L.L. Thurstone, *The Measurement of Values* (Chicago: University of Chicago Press, 1959), esp. 159-210.

10. R. Schlaifer, *Analysis of Decisions Under Uncertainty* (New York: McGraw-Hill, 1969), Chapter 2, "Systematic Analysis of Decisions Under Uncertainty" (pp. 30-83).

Chapter 4
Data Collection

1. G. Polya, in *Patterns of Plausible Inference*, vol. 2 (Princeton, N.J.: Princeton University Press, 1968), points out that operationalization is not

160

merely necessary to the behavioral sciences, but also to the "exact" science of physics (p. 117).

2. G.C. Helmstadter, *Research Concepts in Human Behavior* (New York: Appleton-Century-Crofts/Meredith, 1970), pp. 112-113. B. Skinner, "The Operational Analysis of Psychological Terms," in H. Feigl and M. Brodbeck, eds., *Readings in the Philosophy of Science* (New York: Appleton, 1953), p. 586.

3. R.K. Merton, "On Sociological Theories of the Middle Range," in *On Theoretical Sociology* (New York: The Free Press, 1967), p. 40. R. Bierstedt, in *The Social Order*, 3rd ed. (New York: McGraw-Hill, 1970), discusses Merton's distinction between manifest and latent functions (pp. 305-306). D.R. Hampton, S.E. Summer, and R.A. Webber, in *Organizational Behavior and the Practice of Management*, rev. ed. (Glenview, Ill.: Scott, Foresman, 1973), state that "controls, rules, and patterns of reward sometimes displace goals" (p. 614).

4. G. Lindzey and E. Aronson, eds., *The Handbook of Social Psychology*, 2nd ed., 2 vols. (Reading, Mass.: Addison-Wesley, 1968); J. Guilford, *Psychometric Methods*, 2nd ed. (New York: McGraw-Hill, 1954); N. Gage, ed., *Handbook of Research* (Skokie, Ill.: Rand McNally, 1963); E. Willems and H. Raush, eds., *Naturalistic Viewpoints in Psychological Research* (New York: Holt, Rinehart & Winston, 1969); R. Brandt, *Studying Behavior in Natural Settings* (New York: Holt, Rinehart & Winston, 1972); E. Borgatta, "Analysis of Social Interaction: Actual, Role Playing, and Projective " *Journal of Abnormal, and Social Psychology* 51 (1955):394-405; J. Robinson and P. Shaver, *Measures of Social Psychological Attitudes* (Ann Arbor: Institute for Social Research/University of Michigan, 1968); R. Kahn, *The Dynamics of Interviewing* (New York: Wiley, 1957); *Interviewers' Manual* (Ann Arbor: Institute for Social Research/ University of Michigan, 1969); Claire Seltiz, M. Jahoda, M. Deutsch, and S. Cook, *Research Methods in Social Relations*, rev. ed. (New York: Holt, Rinehart & Winston, 1961); M. Parten, *Surveys, Polls and Samples* (New York: Harper & Row, 1950); L. Festinger and D. Katz, eds., *Research Methods in the Behavioral Sciences* (New York: Holt, Rinehart & Winston, 1966). Most of the above works have good bibliographies that extend the inquiry farther. See also E. Webb, D.T. Campbell, R.D. Schwartz and L. Sechrest, *Unobtrusive Measures* (Chicago, Ill.: Rand McNally, 1966); and G. Allport, *The Use of Personal Documents in Psychological Science* (New York: Social Science Research Council, 1942).

5. R. Thom, *Structural Stability and Morphogenesis*, trans. D.H. Fowler (Reading, Mass.: W.A. Benjamin/Addison-Wesley, 1974). See also Donald T. Campbell and Julian C. Stanley, *Experimental and Quasi-Experimental Designs for Research* (Chicago: Rand McNally, 1966).

6. G. Coombs, "Theory and Methods of Social Measurement," in L. Festinger and D. Katz, eds., *Research Methods in the Behavioral Sciences* (New York: Holt, Rinehart & Winston, 1966), p. 477.

7. Helmstadter, *Research Concepts in Human Behavior*, pp. 265-267.

8. See L. Thurstone and E. Chave, *The Measurement of Attitudes* (Chicago: University of Chicago Press, 1929).

9. Guilford, *Psychometric Methods*, Chapter 11; D. Lewis, *Quantitative Methods in Psychology* (New York: McGraw-Hill, 1960); and E. Lindquist, ed., *Educational Measurement* (Washington, D.C.: American Council on Measurement, 1951).

10. R. Likert, "A Technique for the Measurement of Attitudes," *Archives of Psychology* 140 (1932); L. Thurstone and E. Chave, *The Measurement of Attitude* (Chicago: University of Chicago Press, 1929); and L. Guttman, "A Basis for Scaling Qualitative Data," *Psychometrika* 10 (1945):255-282.

11. *Mental Measurement Yearbook* (Highland Park, N.J.: Gryphon Press, published annually); J. Robinson, J. Rusk, and K. Head, *Measures of Political Attitudes* Ann Arbor: Institute for Social Research/University of Michigan, 1968); J. Robinson and P. Shaver, *Measures of Social Psychological Attitudes*; and M. Shaw and J. Wright, *Scales for the Measurement of Attitudes* (New York: McGraw-Hill, 1967). See also the indexes of all the professional academic journals, and the professional academic compendiums of abstracts.

The various encyclopedias in the behavioral sciences are also valuable sources, such as: C. Harris and M. Liba, eds., *Encyclopedia of Educational Research*, 3rd ed. (New York: Macmillan, 1960). However, for a more restrained view of testing and scaling methods to temper possible overenthusiasm of inventors and users of psychometric instruments, see R.D. Bock and L.V. Jones, *The Measurement and Prediction of Judgment and Choice* (San Francisco: Holden-Day, 1968); another in this area is G.C. Helmstadter, *Research Concepts in Human Behavior*, pp. 265-267.

12. A more complex typology of errors can be found in J. Mursell, *Psychological Testing* (New York: David McKay, 1947).

13. Fritz Roethlisberger and William Dickson, *Management and the Worker* (Cambridge, Mass.: Harvard University Press, 1939). See also, Robert Rosenthal, *Experimenter Effects in Behavioral Research* (New York: Appleton-Century-Crofts, 1966).

Chapter 5
Data Analysis: Descriptive

1. The following discussion is adapted from V. Senders, *Measurement and Statistics* (New York: Oxford University Press, 1958).

2. F.P. Brooks, Jr., and K.E. Iverson, *Automatic Data Processing* (New York: Wiley, 1969); B. Luskin, T. Tilton, and R. Brightman, *Data Processing for Decision-Making* (New York: Macmillan, 1968); and Richard W. Brightman, *Information Systems for Modern Management* (New York: Macmillan, 1971).

3. The Southeast Regional Data Center, located at the Florida International University in Miami, lists a catalogue of 1021 interactive programs as of June 20, 1975.

4. Academic Computing Center, University of Wisconsin at Madison, *STAT-PACK Programmer Reference* (New York: Sperry-Rand, 1973).

5. A more advanced, and difficult, exposition is in Daniel E. Bailey, *Probability and Statistics* (New York: Wiley, 1971), pp. 365 ff.

Chapter 6
Data Analysis: Inferential

1. H. Raiffa, *Decision Analysis: Introductory Lectures on Choices Under Uncertainty* (Reading, Mass.: Addison-Wesley, 1970), pp. 7-38.

2. F. Mosteller and D.L. Wallace, 'Deciding Authorship," pp. 164-175, in J.M. Tavur, F. Mosteller, W.H. Korskal, R.F. Link, R.S. Pieters, G.R. Rising, eds., *Statistics: A Guide to the Unknown* (San Francisco: Holden-Day, 1972). Mosteller and Wallace's *Inference and Disputed Authorship: The Federalist* treats several aspects of content analysis (Reading, Mass.: Addison-Wesley, 1964).

3. S. Richmond, *Statistical Analysis* (New York: Ronald Press, 1964).

4. M. Turner, *Philosophy and the Science of Behavior* (New York: Appleton, 1967).

5. Daniel E. Bailey, *Probability and Statistics* (New York: Wiley, 1971), pp. 327-344. D. Bakan, "The Test of Significance in Psychological Research," *Psychological Bulletin* 66 (December 1966):423-437.

6. M.E. Stern, *Mathematics for Management* (Englewood Cliffs, N.J.: Prentice-Hall, 1963), pp. 412-413.

7. W.C. Guenther, *Concepts of Statistical Inference* (New York: McGraw-Hill, 1965).

8. Bailey, pp. 202-206.

9. Bailey, pp. 197, 244.

10. A. Treloar, *Biometric Analysis: An Introduction* (Minneapolis: Burgess, 1951), p. 156; and R.P. Runyon and A. Haber, *Fundamentals of Behavioral Statistics* (Reading, Mass.: Addison-Wesley, 1972), p. 199.

11. J. Von Neuman and J. Morgenstern, *Theory of Games and Economic Behavior* (New York: Wiley, 1947), is the classic work in this field. There are countless lesser and easier works.

12. M.D. Davis, *Game Theory: A Nontechnical Introduction* (New York: Basic Books, 1970); and R. Schlaifer, *Analysis of Decisions Under Uncertainty* (New York: McGraw-Hill, 1969), pp. v, 3-133.

13. See Von Neuman and Morgenstern, and M.D. Davis.

Chapter 7
Computer Printouts

1. There are many different languages to talk to a computer. Each such programming language is adapted to a certain perspective. The languages can be classified as machine-oriented, procedure-oriented, and problem-oriented. See N. Chapin, *Computers: A System Approach* (New York: Van Nostrand, 1971), p. 376.

2. See the bibliography for an extensive listing of works.

3. For a general treatment of computer data processing on a general, nonoperational level, see Richard W. Brightman, *Information Systems for Modern Management* (New York: Macmillan, 1971).

4. For a relatively simple exposition of correlation, see Daniel E. Bailey, *Probability and Statistics* (New York: Wiley, 1971), pp. 532-605. R.P. Runyon and A. Haber, *Fundamentals of Behavioral Statistics* (Reading, Mass.: Addison-Wesley, 1972), pp. 94-109.

Appendix C
How to Write a Research Report

1. Kate L. Turabian, *A Manual for Writers*, 3rd ed. revised (Chicago: University of Chicago Press, 1967).

Bibliography

Bibliography

Chapter 1
The Professional in a World of Research

Braithwaite, R. *Scientific Explanation*. Cambridge: Cambridge University Press, 1955.

Cherry, Colin. *On Human Communication*. Cambridge, Mass.: MIT Press, 1970.

Criminal Statistics. Monograph Series for NIMH. Washington, D.C.: U.S. Government Printing Office, 1970.

Diamond, S. *Information and Error*. New York: Basic Books, 1959.

Glazer, M. *The Research Adventure: Promise and Problems of Field Work*. New York: Random House, 1972.

Nagi, S.Z., and R.G. Corwin. *The Social Contexts of Research*. New York: Wiley-Interscience, 1972.

Norris, K., and J. Vaizey. *The Economics of Research and Technology*. Santa Fe Springs, Calif.: Davlin, 1973.

Osgood, C., G. Suci, and P. Tannenbaum. *The Measurement of Meaning*. Urbana: University of Illinois Press, 1957.

Polanyi, M. *Logic of Liberty*. Chicago: University of Chicago Press, 1951.

Przeworski, A., and H. Teune. *The Logic of Comparative Social Inquiry*. New York: Wiley, 1970.

Seitz, Frederick. *Science, Government and the Universities*. Seattle: University of Washington Press, 1966.

Symposium on Basic Research. Washington: American Society for the Advancement of Science/Scholastic Reprints, 1959.

Task Force Report: Crime and Its Impact—An Assessment. Report to President's Commission on Law Enforcement and the Administration of Justice. Washington, D.C.: U.S. Government Printing Office, 1967.

Task Force Report: Science and Technology. Report to President's Commission on Law Enforcement and Administration of Justice. Washington, D.C.: U.S. Government Printing Office, 1967.

Thorwald, J. *Crime and Science*. New York: Harcourt, Brace & World, 1967.

Turner, M. *Philosophy and the Science of Behavior*. New York: Appleton-Century-Crofts, 1967.

Zuckerman, S. *Beyond the Ivory Tower: The Frontiers of Public and Private Science*. New York: Taplinger, 1971.

Chapter 2
Scientific Inquiry into Criminal Justice

Lorge, I. "The Fundamental Nature of Measurement." In E. Lindquist, ed., *Educational Measurement*. Washington, D.C.: American Council on Measurement, 1951.

Michalos, Alex C. *Principles of Logic.* Englewood Cliffs, N.J.: Prentice-Hall, 1969.

Neale, John M., and Robert M. Liebert. *Science and Behavior.* Englewood Cliffs, N.J.: Prentice-Hall, 1973.

Ross, R. *Research: An Introduction.* New York: Barnes & Noble, 1974.

Stover, C.F. *The Government of Science.* Santa Barbara, Calif.: Center for the Study of Democratic Institutions, 1962.

Yovits, Marshall C., ed. *Research Program Effectiveness.* New York: Gordon, 1966.

*Typical Applications of Science to
Current Problems*

Greenwood, P.W., and J. Petersilia. *The Criminal Investigation Process*, 3 vols. Santa Monica, Calif.: Rand, 1975.

Kelling, George L., Tony Pate, Duane Dieckman, and Charles E. Brown. *The Kansas City Preventive Patrol Experiment: Final Report.* Washington, D.C.: Police Foundation, 1974.

**Chapter 3
Research Design**

Blalock, H.M. Jr. *An Introduction to Social Research.* Englewood Cliffs, N.J.: Prentice-Hall, 1970.

Campbell, D. and J. Stanley. *Experimental and Quasi-Experimental Design for Research.* (Skokie, Ill.: Rand McNally, 1963.

Festinger, L., and D. Katz, eds. *Research Methods in the Behavioral Sciences.* New York: Holt, Rinehart & Winston, 1966.

Forcese, D.P., and S. Richer. *Social Research Methods.* Englewood Cliffs, N.J.: Prentice-Hall, 1973.

Helmstadter, G.C. *Research Concepts in Human Behavior.* New York: Appleton-Century-Crofts, 1970.

Holt, R.T., and J.E. Turner, eds. *The Methodology of Comparative Political Research.* New York: Free Press, 1970.

Kerlinger, Fred N. *Foundations of Behavioral Research*, 2nd ed. New York: Holt, Rinehart & Winston, 1973.

Leedy, Paul D. *Practical Research: Planning and Design.* New York: Macmillan, 1974.

Lloyd, L.E. *Techniques for Efficient Research.* New York: Chemical Publishing, 1966.

Lothrop, W.C. *Paradoxes in Research Administration.* Ann Arbor: University of Michigan Press, 1959.

McLoughlin, S.G. *Fundamentals of Research Management*. Chicago: American Management Association, 1971.

Nolting, B.E. *Art of Research*. New York: Elsevier, 1965.

Paradis, A.A. *The Research Handbook*. Chicago: Funk and Wagnalls, 1974.

Miller, Delbert C. *Handbook of Research Design and Social Measurement*. New York: David McKay, 1970.

Sidman, M. *Tactics of Scientific Research*. New York: Basic Books, 1960.

Smith, H.W. *Strategies of Social Research: The Methodological Imagination*. Englewood Cliffs, N.J.: Prentice-Hall, 1975.

Steele, H.C. *How to Motivate and Direct Students in Science Research*. Huntsville, Ala.: Strode, 1970.

Tullock, G. *Organization of Inquiry*. Durham, N.C.: Duke University Press, 1966.

Wilson, E. *Introduction to Scientific Research*. New York: McGraw-Hill, 1952.

Wirt, John G., Arnold J. Lieberman, and Roger E. Levien. *R & D Management: Methods Used by Federal Agencies*. Lexington, Mass.: Lexington Books, D.C. Heath, 1975.

Chapter 4
Data Collection

The collection of data of physical attributes is considered to be much simpler than of human qualities, or aspects of human personality. Thus these references give most attention to the latter.

Babbie, Earl R. *Survey Research Methods*. Belmont, Calif.: Wadsworth, 1973.

Cartwright, D., and A. Zander, eds. *Group Dynamics*. New York: Harper & Row, 1958.

Committee on Historiography. *Theory and Practice in Historical Study*. New York: Social Science Research Council, 1946.

Guildford, J. *Psychometric Methods,* 2nd ed. New York: McGraw-Hill, 1954.

Nunnally, J. *Psychometric Theory*. New York: McGraw-Hill, 1967.

Rivers, Wendell L. *Finding Facts: Interviewing, Observing, Using Reference Sources*. Englewood Cliffs, N.J.: Prentice-Hall, 1975.

Rosen, L., and R. West. *Reader for Research Methods*. New York: Random House, 1973.

Thurstone, L. and E. Chave. *The Measurement of Attitude*. Chicago: University of Chicago Press, 1929.

Wallace, D. "A Case for and Against Mail Questionnaires." *Public Opinion Quarterly* 18 (1954):40-52.

Webb, E., D. Campbell, R. Schwartz, and L. Sechrest. *Unobtrusive Measures: Non-Reactive Research in the Social Sciences*. Chicago: Rand McNally, 1966.

White, R. *Value-Analysis: The Nature and Use of the Method.* New York: Society for the Psychological Study of Social Issues, 1951.

Chapter 5
Data Analysis: Descriptive

Blank, S.S. *Descriptive Statistics.* New York: Appleton-Century-Crofts, 1968.
Dayton, C.M., and C.L. Stunkard, *Statistics for Problem-Solving.* New York: McGraw-Hill, 1971.
Fisher, R. *The Design of Experiments*, 6th ed. New York: Hafner, 1951.
_____. *Statistical Methods for Research Workers.* New York: Hafner, 1973.
Guilford, J. *Fundamental Studies in Psychology and Education.* New York: McGraw-Hill, 1956.
Hays, W. *Statistics.* New York: Holt, Rinehart & Winston, 1973.
Kemeny, J., et al. *Finite Mathematical Structures.* Englewood Cliffs, N.J.: Prentice-Hall, 1959.
Lohnes, P., and W. Cooley. *Introduction to Statistical Procedures, with Computer Exercises.* New York: Wiley, 1968.
Runyon, R.P., and A. Haber. *Fundamentals of Behavioral Statistics.* Reading, Mass.: Addison-Wesley, 1972.
Tamur, Judith M., Frederick Mosteller, William H. Kruskal, Richard F. Link, Richard S. Pieters, and Gerald R. Rising, eds., *Statistics: A Guide to the Unknown.* San Francisco: Holden-Day, 1972.
Weinberg, George H., and John A. Schumaker. *Statistics: An Intuitive Approach*, 3rd ed. Monterey, Calif.: Brooks/Cole, 1974.

Chapter 6
Data Analysis: Inferential

Cooley, W., and P. Lohnes. *Multivariate Data Analysis.* New York: Wiley, 1971.
Fisher, R. *Statistical Method and Scientific Inference.* London: Oliver & Boyd, 1959.
Harman, H. *Modern Factor Analysis.* Chicago: University of Chicago Press, 1960.
Horst, P. *Factor Analysis of Data Matrices.* New York: Holt, Rinehart & Winston, 1941.
Kerlinger, F., and E. Pedhazur. *Multiple Regression in Behavioral Research.* New York: Holt, Rinehart & Winston, 1973.
Raiffa, H. *Decision Analysis: Introductory Lectures on Choices Under Uncertainty.* Reading, Mass.: Addison-Wesley, 1970.
Richmond, S. *Statistical Analysis.* New York: Ronald Press, 1964.

Willmer, M.A.P. *Crime and Information Theory.* Edinburgh: Edinburgh University Press, 1976.

Chapter 7
Computer Printouts

Bassler, R., and E.O. Joslin. *Applications of Computer Systems.* Arlington, Va.: College Readings, 1974.

Besher, H. *Computer Methods in the Analysis of Large-Scale Social Systems.* Cambridge, Mass.: Joint Center for Urban Studies, MIT and Harvard University, 1965.

General Information Manual: Introduction to IBM Data Processing Systems. Poughkeepsie, N.Y.: IBM Corporation, 1975.

Janda, K. *Data Processing,* 2nd ed. Evanston, Ill.: Northwestern University Press, 1969.

Joslin, E.O. *Computer Readings for Making It Count.* Arlington, Va.: College Readings, 1974.

Klecka, William R., Norman H. Nie, and C. Hadlai Hull. *SPSS Primer: Statistical Package for the Social Sciences.* New York: McGraw-Hill, 1975.

Kossack, C.F., and A. Henschke. *Introduction to Statistics and Computer Programming.* San Francisco: Holden-Day, 1975.

Nie, Norman H., C. Hadlai Hull, Jean G. Jenkins, Karin Steinbrenner, and Dale H. Brent. *Statistical Package for the Social Sciences,* 2nd ed. New York: McGraw-Hill, 1975.

Sack, John, and Judith Meadows. *Entering Basic.* Chicago: Science Research Associates, 1973.

STATJOB Series. Madison: Academic Computing Center, University of Wisconsin, 1976.

General References

The above list does not even skim the surface of the available literature. In reaching across the boundaries of the disciplines, it is appropriate to examine the research literature of all types. The following have been unusually productive of ideas that have been found to be transferable to criminal justice:

Lindzey, G., and E. Aronson, eds. *The Handbook of Social Psychology,* 2nd ed., 2 vols. Reading, Mass.: Addison-Wesley, 1968.

Thorndike, R., ed. *Educational Measurement,* 2nd ed. Washington, D.C.: American Council on Education, 1971.

A useful book on graphs and graphical analysis is:

Cameron, A.J. *A Guide to Graphs.* London: Pergamon Press, 1970.

For more assistance in preparing research proposals:

Leedy, Paul. *Practical Research.* New York: Macmillan, 1974.

For more information about running a research project, controlling it, and evaluating it:

Adams, Stuart. *Evaluative Research in Corrections.* Washington, D.C.: U.S. Government Printing Office, 1975.

Allbright, Ellen, Martin A. Baum, Brenda Forman, Sol Gems, David Jaffe, Frank C. Jordan, Jr., Ruth Katz, and Philip A. Sinsky. *Criminal Justice Research: Evaluation in CRJ Programs.* Washington, D.C.: U.S. Government Printing Office, 1974.

Bush, G.P., and L. Hattery, eds. *Teamwork in Research.* Seattle: University Press of Washington, 1953.

Criminal Justice Evaluation: An Annotated Bibliography. Washington, D.C.: U.S. Department of Justice, NILECR, 1975.

Intensive Evaluation for Criminal Justice Planning Agencies. Washington, D.C.: U.S. Department of Justice, NILECR, 1976.

Frederiksen, N. *Organizational Climates and Administrative Performance.* Princeton, N.J.: Educational Testing Service, 1968.

Jitendra, S., ed. *Management of Scientific Research.* New York: International Publications, 1974.

Lipetz, B. *Measurement of Efficiency of Scientific Research.* New York: Intermedia, 1965.

Suchman, Edward A. *Evaluative Research, Principles and Practice in Public Service and Social Action Programs.* New York: Russell Sage Foundation, 1967.

Viano, Emilio, ed. *Criminal Justice Research.* Lexington, Mass.: Lexington Books, D.C. Heath, 1975.

Weidman, Donald R., John D. Waller, Dona MacNeil, Francine L. Tolson, Joseph S. Wholey. *Intensive Evaluation for Criminal Justice Planning Agencies.* Washington, D.C.: U.S. Department of Justice, NILECR, 1975.

Weiss, Carol H. *Evaluation Research.* Englewood Cliffs, N.J.: Prentice-Hall, 1972.

The matter of sources of data, and of information, is the foundation of all research. The prime source is the labor of the researcher. Secondary sources are in various repositories, books, and data banks of one kind or another.

Government offices are chock full; private corporations, if accessible, sometimes have valuable data resources. The greatest single source of records, available by simple order, is the Criminal Justice Reference Service in Washington, D.C. The other offices of the Department of Justice are good, as are the National Technical Service of the Department of Commerce; the Department of Transportation, the National Institute of Mental Health, and many others. Here are some reference works:

Brimmer, B. *Guide to the Use of United Nations Documents.* New York: Oceana, 1962.

Cook, M.G. *New Library Key*, 3rd ed. New York: Wilson, 1975.

Chandler, G. *How to Find Out.* New York: Pergamon Press, 1974.

Directory of Graduate Research. New York: American Chemical Society, 1971.

Document Retrieval Index. National Criminal Justice Document Retrieval Index (yearly). Washington, D.C.: U.S. Department of Justice, LEAA, NCJR Service.

Dossick, J.J. *Doctoral Research at the School of Education*, New York University, 1890-1970, A Classified Bibliography with critical and statistical analysis. New York: New York University Press, 1972.

Gates, J.K. *Guide to the Use of Books and Libraries*, 3rd ed. New York: McGraw-Hill, 1974.

Hoffman, H.R. *The Reader's Advisor*, 10th ed. New York: R.R. Bowker, 1964.

Joffe, I. *Locating Specific Information.* New York: Wadsworth, 1971.

Lipetz, B. *Guide to Case Studies of Scientific Activity.* New York: Intermedia, 1965.

Mason, J.B., ed. *Research Resources*, 2 vols. New York: ABC-Olio, 1968.

Palmer, A.M., ed. *New Research Centers Directory*, 5th ed. Detroit: Gale Research, 1974.

Rothenberg, A., and B. Greenberg. *The Index of Scientific Writings on Creativity*, 2 vols. New York: Archon, 1976.

Schmeckebier, L., and R. Eastin. *Government Publications and Their Use*, 2nd ed. Washington, D.C.: Brookings Institution, 1961.

Short, R.W., and R. DeMaria, eds. *Subjects and Sources for Research Writing.* New York: Norton, 1963.

Todd, A. *Finding Facts Fast.* New York: Morrow, 1974.

Walker, N. *Crimes, Courts and Figures: An Introduction to Criminal Statistics.* New York: Peter Smith, 1973.

Winchell, C.M. *Guide to Reference Books*, 8th ed. Chicago: American Library Association, 1966.

These books discuss how to read research reports in the various disciplines:

Auger, C.P., ed. *Use of Reports Literature.* New York: Archon, 1975.

Huck, A. *Reading Statistics and Research.* New York: Harper & Row, 1974.

Leaver, R.H., and T.R. Thomas. *Analysis and Presentation of Experimental Results.* New York: Halsted Press, 1975.

The following works deal with research funding:

Committee on Science and Public Policy. *Federal Support of Basic Research in Institutions of Higher Learning.* Washington, D.C.: National Academy of Science, 1964.

Strickland, S., ed. *Sponsored Research in American Universities.* New York: A.C.E., 1968.

When undertaking to find research reports on a given subject, it is often helpful to obtain a general review, such as given in journals, usually those with the word "review" in their title, e.g., the *Review of Educational Research*, or the *Annual Review of Psychology.*

More reliable summaries of current research can be found in abstracting publications, because often the abstracts are prepared by the original research author himself, e.g., *Dissertation Abstracts*, published monthly by University Microfilms, Ann Arbor, Michigan.

The various professional journals in all major disciplines are valuable resources. There are a number of directories of periodicals (Ulrichs International Periodical Directory is a good one) which list periodicals in the various disciplines. Some of the periodicals of particular relevance to criminal justice are: *Abstracts on Criminology and Penology, American Criminal Law Review, American Criminologist, American Journal of Correction, American Journal of Criminal Law, Canadian Journal of Criminology and Corrections, Corrections Digest, Crime and Delinquency, Crime and Delinquency Literature, Crime Control Digest, Criminal Justice Newsletter, Criminal Law Digest* (Supplement), *Criminal Law Quarterly, Criminal Law Reporter, Criminal Law Review* (London), *Criminology, Drug Enforcement, FBI Law Enforcement Bulletin, Federal Probation, Journal of Criminal Justice, Journal of Criminal Law and Criminology, Journal of Police Science and Administration, Journal of Research in Crime and Delinquency, Juvenile Justice, Law and Society Review, Prison Journal, The Police Chief.* It will be noted that not many of them even promise research reportage. They illustrate, however, the state-of-the-art. There are many others to choose from.

Often when a research report is overly long, it will be published serially in monograph form. A number of such supplementary materials, particularly in psychology and education, can provide useful background to criminal justice professionals in particular subject areas.

The Foundation Center, 888 7th Avenue, New York 10019, provides many services, and publications on private funding for research.

Index

Index

177

About the Author

Robert S. Clark received the Ph.D. degree in political science from New York University. He is Associate Professor of Criminal Justice at Florida International University in Miami. He is the author of many articles on monitoring information, legitimacy of authority, grand juries and scientific research. At the present time Dr. Clark conducts a column, "Guidelines in Scientific Research" for the journal of the International Association of Chiefs of Police, *The Police Chief.* He is the author of two books on research, *Criminal Justice Research: Guidelines for Professionals*, and *Scientific Research.* Dr. Clark's approach to criminal justice research is laced with a pragmatism founded in a background of two decades with the New York City Police Department, and as a lawyer-investigator in agency work. The locale of his research has included the United States and many of the countries of Europe.